Success
STRATEGIES

CelebrityPress®
Winter Park, Florida

CONTENTS

CHAPTER 1

THE ONE STRATEGY THAT CHANGES EVERYTHING

BY JACK CANFIELD

The indispensible first step to getting the things
you want out of life is this: decide what you want.
~ Ben Stein
Writer, actor and social commentator

One of the greatest myths in this world is that we're entitled to live a great life. That somehow, somewhere—someone—is required to fill our lives with continual happiness, exciting career options, empowering personal opportunities, and blissful relationships simply because we exist on this planet. We expect these things—and when they don't show up, for many of us at least, it's someone else's fault.

But perhaps the greatest truth in this world—and the one lesson you must learn in order to be successful—is that there's only one person responsible for the life you enjoy here.

That person is YOU.

If you want to be successful, you have to take 100% responsibility for everything you experience in your life—from the level of your achievements to the results you produce, to the quality of your relationships, to the state of your health and physical fitness... even responsibility for your feelings, your income, your debts... everything!

You have to do those things that will bring you the life that you want. You have to stop blaming—your parents, your spouse, other people, the economy, your boss—for the way things are, and you have to stop complaining about how you wish things were different.

DECIDE WHAT SUCCESS MEANS TO YOU

Of course, the biggest step toward taking responsibility for your future is to decide what "success" looks like for you.

You must decide what you want.

Unfortunately, most people bungle this crucial first step because they simply can't see how it's possible to get what they want—so they don't even let themselves want it.

I can't earn a living doing that, they say. Or worse: I'm not good enough, smart enough, or pretty enough. I don't know the right people, the best way to start, where the money will come from, or when I would find the time.

But one of the most amazing phenomena you'll ever experience once you decide what you want, is the unexpected phone call, the windfall financial benefit or the uncanny new acquaintance that brings you exactly what you want or need in order to achieve your loftiest goals—almost as if it were planned.

Perhaps it's the Universe, rewarding your new decision and take-action attitude by harnessing all the forces at its disposal. Or perhaps you've worked hard and have "grown" yourself to the point where you're finally ready to receive a benefit which had been waiting in the wings all along.

But more probably, as researchers have now come to believe, it may simply be a matter of your subconscious mind focusing on and recognizing opportunity when it arrives.

Whatever the explanation, the reality is that what you want, wants you.

Your goals, desires and needs are patiently waiting to gravitate toward you, once you decide what you truly want.

Of course, the main reason why most people don't get what they want is they haven't decided what that "want" is. They haven't defined their goals—exactly—in clear and compelling detail. After all, how else can your mind know where to begin looking, seeing and hearing if you don't give it specific and detailed goals to achieve?

Clarify Your Vision and Your Values

There's a very powerful technique I want to teach you for helping you define your goals in vivid, colorful and compelling detail. But before using this technique to write down your goals—before defining the compelling life you want for yourself—you must first know what your priorities are. Priorities are "wants" that are personally important to you—not those you believe should be important or those you think the world expects you to value—but what's truly important to you from the deepest place in your heart.

Once you know your "wants," you must also determine your core values. What kinds of activities and priorities are in alignment with your integrity? Which are outside your acceptable limits?

Think about it. You might "want" all the riches and material wealth that could come from selling illegal drugs, but you might find it very difficult to convince your mind and body of your enthusiasm, especially if breaking the law and contributing to broken lives went against your basic values. In fact, engaging in an activity you don't agree with often causes low self-esteem, depression, despondency, or even anger. So be sure that what you want matches your values.

Don't Live Someone Else's Dream

Be certain, too, that what you "want" isn't someone else's version of what you should want.

I once met an anesthesiologist who made $350,000 a year, but whose real dream was to work on cars. He had wanted to be a mechanic, but he knew his mother wouldn't approve. My solution? "Give yourself permission to buy a bunch of cars and then work on them on the weekends," I said. What the anesthesiologist wanted in his heart didn't match his picture of what he thought he should be.

Unfortunately, the sad reality for most people is they simply aren't honest with themselves. If they were, they would realize their "want to's" are almost always bigger than their "shoulds."

Is "Making a Living" Stopping You?

Of course, what often stops people from expressing their true desire is that they don't think they can make a living doing what they love to do.

"What I love to do is hang out and talk with people," you might say.

Well, Oprah Winfrey—plus countless other talk show hosts and podcasters—have made fortunes hanging out and talking with people. And my friend Diane Brause, who is an international tour director, makes a living hanging out talking with people in some of the most exciting cities in the world.

See how it's possible to make a great living doing what you want to do? You simply have to be willing to risk it.

THE SEVEN AREAS OF GREATEST IMPACT

If you were lucky growing up, you were encouraged to dream big about who you wanted to be when you were older—and what you wanted to have and enjoy during your lifetime. For many of us though, as children our dreams were ignored, or we were told they were silly—or worse, that we would never amount to much. Many of us put aside what we truly wanted in order to get along or avoid conflict. Then as we became adults, we were told to be practical and realistic.

But what about now?

While you may have had to adapt to survive back then, you now know that a bigger, more exciting life is available to you. This is your chance to break free of any negative childhood programming and the adult requirement of "being practical," and expand your sense of what's possible, to dream once more, and to envision what you truly want in all the areas of your life.

One of the easiest ways to begin deciding what you truly want is to make an "I-Want" list. You can do this exercise alone or enroll a friend to help you. For 10-15 minutes, have your friend continually ask, *What do you want? What do you want?* while they write down your answers.

You'll find the first "wants" aren't all that profound. In fact, most people usually hear themselves saying, "I want a Lamborghini. I want a big house at the beach. I want to retire early." But by the end of the exercise, the real you begins to speak, *I want people to love me. I want to express myself. I want to make a difference. I want to feel powerful…*wants that are true expressions of your core values.

Visualize What You Want

While jotting down what you want may be the first time you've ever sat down to dream about your ideal future life, there's another—even more powerful—way to succeed in achieving what you want to be, do, and have: visualizing what your successful life would look like in the major areas or categories of your life that can literally change *everything* about who you are, what you do, and how you live right now.

Below are seven major life categories where most of our dreams, goals and achievements live. To truly master the first step toward tremendous success, set aside a few hours to really think about what you truly want in each category—a*nd why you want it.* Why is retiring early important to you? Why do you want to live in a million-dollar home? Why do you want to begin studying another language? Will it improve your lifestyle, give you joy, allow you to help others, or something else?

Decide what you want to be, do and have—*and why you want that.*

But most importantly, don't hold back when thinking about what you want. Give yourself permission to list anything and everything that comes to mind. Don't edit your dreams because they're too expensive, too difficult, different from anything you've ever done before, or "not acceptable" to your family and friends. No one else needs to approve what you write—or even see it. This is for YOU. Dream big!

Visualize Your Finances

Begin this exercise by listening to some relaxing music and sitting quietly in a comfortable environment. Then, start visualizing your ideal life exactly as if you are living it.

First, visualize your financial situation. How much money do you have in your savings? How much income do you make? What is your net worth? How is your cash flow? How much is in your retirement account?

Visualize Your Possessions

Next, visualize what your dream house—your "forever home"— would look like. What style of house is it? Where is it located? What color is the interior? How is it furnished? Are there paintings on the walls? What do they look like? Walk through your perfect house visually, using your mind's eye.

At this point, don't worry about how you'll get that house. Don't sabotage yourself by thinking or saying, *I can't live in Hawaii because I don't make enough money.* Once you give your mind's eye the picture, your subconscious mind will solve the "not enough money" challenge. Simply be honest with yourself about what you truly want. Continue visualizing your perfect home. Does it include extensive property, gardens, stables, unique views, a pool, a tennis court, a guesthouse, an art studio or any other unique characteristics?

Next, visualize what kind of car you are driving, followed by any other possessions you'd like to acquire. Do you own a boat? Where is it harbored? Do you have valuable artwork, an extensive library, designer or antique furnishings, important art objects or unique collectibles?

Visualize Your Work, Career or Business

Next, visualize what you are doing in your career. Where are you working? Who are you working with? What is your compensation like? Is it your own business? What kind of clients do you have?

Have you pursued higher education and earned a degree or a certification? Are you in management, outreach, advocacy, or some other unique role?

Visualize Your Relationships

Move on to visualizing the perfect relationships you want in your life. What is the quality of your relationships with your family? Who are your friends? What do those friendships feel like? Are they loving, supportive, and empowering? What activities are you doing with your friends? How are your needs getting met in your relationships?

Visualize Your Fun Time

Next, focus on your rest, relaxation and recreation time. What are you doing with your family and friends in the free time you've created for yourself? What hobbies are you pursuing? What kinds of vacations do you take? Are you traveling to exotic locales? Are you spending a month or two in a specific place?

Visualize Your Health and Fitness

Then, visualize your ideal body, your physical health, and your emotional state. Are you free and open, relaxed, and in an ecstatic state of happiness all day long? What does that look and feel like?

What are you doing to stay fit and healthy? What kinds of foods are you eating and how are they prepared? Are you practicing daily exercise, meditation, yoga, tai chi, mindfulness or some other regular practice?

Visualize Your Personal and Spiritual Growth

What about your own personal growth? Do you see yourself going back to school, taking training, seeking therapy for a past hurt or otherwise growing in confidence? Are you working with a coach? Are you in a mastermind group? Are you actively pursuing a spiritual life including belonging to a church, pursuing religious education or daily study, traveling to sacred places, or volunteering for missions work?

THE ONE STRATEGY THAT CHANGES EVERYTHING

Visualize Making a Difference and Being of Service

Finally, think about the "community" you've chosen to live in. It might be a geographic location or a community of like-minded people scattered around the world. What does it look like? What kinds of activities take place?

Think about being of service to others. What charitable or philanthropic work are you pursuing? What are you doing to make a difference? How often do you participate in these activities? Who are you helping? How are their lives being changed?

Share Your Vision for Maximum Impact

Finally, when you've created a vivid picture in your mind and written down the details of the life you want, share your vision with somebody. This can be very uncomfortable. In fact, most people believe, *I can't share that! It's too personal. What I want is crazy. People will think I'm too selfish, too woo-woo, or too weird.* But the truth is that most of the people you talk to will want many of the same things.

Everyone wants material wealth, loving relationships, supportive family and friends, and time to help make a difference in our world. But too few of us readily admit it. Sharing your vision will help your subconscious mind become more accountable to making it happen.

CREATE A VISION OF YOUR SUCCESSFUL LIFE

Now that you've created a wish list of your ideal life, it's time to create tangible pictures for your brain to focus on. As scientists now know, the brain is a goal-seeking organism. Visualizing your dreams and goals as already complete—which focuses the brain on success—may be the most underutilized success tool that you possess. It can greatly accelerate the attainment of any goal in three powerful ways:

1. Visualization activates the creative powers of the subconscious mind to come up with solutions you may have never thought of before.
2. Visualization "programs" the brain's reticular activating system to sift through the millions of impressions you receive every day and notice new resources and opportunities (or resources that were always there) that can be used to achieve your goals. Visualization focuses the brain on solutions.
3. Visualization magnetizes and attracts to you the people, resources, and "lucky breaks" you need to achieve your goals.

None of us learned about visualization in school. But in the last 30 years, sports psychologists and peak performance experts have been popularizing the power of visualization. Today, nearly all Olympic and professional athletes employ the power of visualization.

Interestingly, most of us unwittingly use visualization on a daily basis, but too often, we do it without thinking—and in a negative fashion.

I'm talking about *worrying*.

What happens to our bodies when we worry? We tense up, disrupt our normal breathing, and psycho-physically prepare ourselves for failure. But by *instead* using positive visualization to prepare yourself for success, you will transform the energy that supports your worrying into fuel for making your dreams come true.

The process of visualizing for success is really quite simple. All you need to do is close your eyes and visualize your goals and objectives as already complete.

If one of your goals is to own a nice house on the lake, then simply close your eyes and see yourself walking through the exact house you would like to own. Fill in all of the details. What does the exterior look like? How is it landscaped? What kind of view does it have? What does the living room, kitchen, master bedroom, dining room, great room and sunroom look like? How is it furnished? Go from room to room and fill in all of the details. Is there a workshop, mudroom, cabana, guest house, pool or spa?

Make the images as clear and as bright as possible. Take the time to use the power of your creative mind to create vivid images of your goal.

The first time you create the image it will take a few minutes to fill in all the details. After that, each time you revisit the image, it will only take a few seconds to call up all of the images you've already created. It will be more like looking at a video or a Pinterest board that you've already created.

Repeat this process for every goal that you have. Refer to the "wants" you listed above in the seven key areas of your life. Many people revisit and upgrade their goals once a year. I suggest that you write each of your goals and objectives for the year—as well as any longer-term goals like financial independence and a vacation home in Hawaii—on a separate 3x5 index card or in your Notes app on your cell phone. Then, each morning when you arise and each night before you go to bed, read through the cards or your list, pausing after each one to close your eyes and recreate the visual image in your mind of that completed goal. Continue through the cards until you have visualized each goal as fulfilled. The whole process will take about five minutes.

If you're in the habit of meditating, you can do this after meditating for maximum benefit.

This daily practice of visualizing your goals as already complete will keep your subconscious mind focused on the realization of your goals. And just like the guidance system on one of the "smart bombs" used in the military, it will keep you on track until you manifest the result.

Add Sounds and Feelings to the Pictures

To add extra fuel and motivational power to the visualization process, be sure to imagine the sights and sounds you would be hearing, plus the emotions and bodily sensations you would be feeling if you had already achieved the goal. The sound of ocean waves breaking onshore…the thrill of winning the contest…your pride of ownership in your new vehicle…your spouse thanking you for being such a good provider—emotions and sounds like these will add impact to the power of visualization.

Create a Vision Board

In addition to visualizing in your mind's eye, you can also use external pictures, images and symbols to keep your conscious and subconscious mind focused on your goals. For example, if one of your goals is to own a new sports car, you can grab your smartphone and go to your local dealer, take a selfie of you leaning against your dream car, or even better, sitting behind the wheel of the car waving out of the driver's side window.

If your goal is to visit Paris, find a beautiful picture of the Eiffel Tower online and Photoshop yourself into the scene—then print and post it where you will see it frequently. I did this with a picture of the Sydney Opera House, and within a year I was hired for a speaking engagement in Sydney, Australia. If your goal is to be a millionaire, you might want to write yourself a check for $1,000,000 or create a printed statement that shows your bank account or 401(k) with a $1,000,000 balance.

If your goal is to have your book reach #1 on the *New York Times* bestseller list, you might want to photocopy the bestseller list, white out the current #1 book, and type your book's title in its place. Or you might want to use your computer to create a newspaper article declaring you the bestselling author of the year. If you're working on reaching your ideal weight, you can photo-edit your head onto a picture of the perfect body that represents your ideal weight or shape.

Once you've created these images, you can mount them—along with photos you've collected of famous places you'd like to visit, private jets, happy children, or any other goal you have—collage-style onto a vision board. Then place your *vision board* somewhere central where you will see it several times a day, such as your office, the kitchen, or the upstairs hall near the stairs where you'll pass by it often.

SET A GOAL THAT WILL HELP YOU ACHIEVE YOUR BIGGEST "WANT"

Once you decide what you want in the seven key areas above, you can turn those dreams into goals to work on—adding specific, measurable details like *how much* and *by when*. When you know *exactly* what to work towards, you can begin to break down these goals into small, achievable steps that add up to completing your goal.

While goal-setting is an important step to achieving success, most of the goals we set focus on improving our life in the moment: lose 20 pounds, save for that vacation, clean out the garage.

But what if—instead—you focused on a single goal that would amplify everything you do...from your career to your acquaintances...to your income...to your lifestyle? Wouldn't that be a goal worth pursuing with passion? Wouldn't that be something to focus on a little each day until you achieved it?

Think about the biggest "want" on your list above. If you were an independent sales professional and knew you could get a better territory, a substantial bonus commission and maybe even a promotion once you landed a certain number of customers, wouldn't you work day and night to achieve that goal? And if you were a stay-at-home parent whose entire family lifestyle and finances would change by earning an extra $1,000 a month, wouldn't you pursue every possible opportunity until you achieved that goal?

That's what I call a "Breakthrough Goal"—one that when you have achieved it, changes your life, brings you new opportunities, gets you in front of the right people and uplevels every activity, relationship or group you're involved in. Whether you believe you can achieve it or not, what one single change in your career, business, lifestyle or relationships would boost you to the next level? Once you know what it is, you can begin visualizing daily how your life would change as a result of accomplishing that goal. What would you be doing, seeing and feeling?

* * * *

Only when you take the time to decide what you truly want— then set goals and visualize your "wants" as already achieved— will you see your successes begin to add up to the life of your dreams.

Remember to dream big. The only limiting factor is your imagination—and your willingness and commitment to take the necessary action to achieve your goals.

About Jack

Known as America's #1 Success Coach, Jack Canfield is the CEO of the Canfield Training Group in Santa Barbara, CA, which trains and coaches entrepreneurs, corporate leaders, managers, sales professionals and the general public in how to accelerate the achievement of their personal, professional and financial goals.

Jack Canfield is best known as the coauthor of the #1 *New York Times* bestselling *Chicken Soup for the Soul®* book series, which has sold more than 500 million books in 47 languages, including 11 *New York Times* #1 bestsellers. As the CEO of Chicken Soup for the Soul Enterprises he helped grow the *Chicken Soup for the Soul®* brand into a virtual empire of books, children's books, audios, videos, CDs, classroom materials, a syndicated column and a television show, as well as a vigorous program of licensed products that includes everything from clothing and board games to nutraceuticals and a successful line of *Chicken Soup for the Pet Lover's Soul®* cat and dog foods.

His other books include *The Success Principles™: How to Get from Where You Are to Where You Want to Be* (recently revised as the 10th Anniversary Edition), *The Success Principles for Teens, The Aladdin Factor, Dare to Win, Heart at Work, The Power of Focus: How to Hit Your Personal, Financial and Business Goals with Absolute Certainty, You've Got to Read This Book, Tapping into Ultimate Success, Jack Canfield's Key to Living the Law of Attraction*, his recent novel, *The Golden Motorcycle Gang: A Story of Transformation* and *The 30-Day Sobriety Solution*.

Jack is a dynamic speaker and was recently inducted into the National Speakers Association's Speakers Hall of Fame. He has appeared on more than 1000 radio and television shows including Oprah, Montel, Larry King Live, The Today Show, Fox and Friends, and 2 hour-long PBS Specials devoted exclusively to his work. Jack is also a featured teacher in 12 movies including *The Secret, The Meta-Secret, The Truth, The Keeper of the Keys, Tapping into the Source*, and *The Tapping Solution*. Jack was also honored recently with a documentary that was produced about his life and teachings, *The Soul of Success: The Jack Canfield Story.*

Jack has personally helped hundreds of thousands of people on six different continents become multi-millionaires, business leaders, best-selling authors, leading sales professionals, successful entrepreneurs, and world-class athletes while at the same time creating balanced, fulfilling and healthy lives.

His corporate clients have included Virgin Records, SONY Pictures, Daimler-Chrysler, Federal Express, GE, Johnson & Johnson, Merrill Lynch, Campbell's Soup, Re/Max, The Million Dollar Forum, The Million Dollar Roundtable, The Young Entrepreneurs Organization, The Young Presidents Organization, the Executive Committee, and the World Business Council.

Jack is the founder of the Transformational Leadership Council and a member of Evolutionary Leaders, two groups devoted to helping create a world that works for everyone.

Jack is a graduate of Harvard, earned his M.Ed. from the University of Massachusetts, and has received three honorary doctorates in psychology and public service. He is married, has three children, two step-children and a grandson.

For more information, visit:
- www.JackCanfield.com
- www.CanfieldTraintheTrainer.com

CHAPTER 2

LIFESAVING SUCCESS STRATEGY: THE ART OF HUMAN CARE

BY HASSAN A. TETTEH, MD

The Art of Human Care is the ultimate lifesaving success strategy. I know this because the art of human care, embodied in purpose, personalization, and partnership, saved my life. At every stage of my medical career, I lost friends and colleagues to burnout, a departure from the profession of medicine, and, in extreme cases, suicide. Friends and colleagues that will never practice the art of human care because of a life cut short. Doctors who will never save a life because no one could help save their life. Twenty years ago, the term, "burnout" was not as well defined or studied as it is today. A 2019 Harvard study by Joel Goh and colleagues determined the problem of burnout was not just a problem impacting physician happiness. Burnout has severe implications for healthcare and costs an estimated $4.6 billion, due to reduced hours, turn over, and the expenses associated with finding and replacing physicians that leave the profession.

Burnout among physicians is roughly double that of the general population and, yet, the root cause of the problem is multifactorial—including emotional exhaustion, feelings of cynicism, detachment from work, and low personal accomplishment. Over the past ten years, I reflected deeply on this subject, thought about my friends and colleagues lost to burnout, depression, and suicide, and created a solution to help address the problem of burnout and engender a renewed passion for healthcare. The sum of my work is *The Art of Human Care*—a philosophy of purpose, personalization, and partnerships that aim to change the world positively. At the root of the art of human care is *art*, because, at my core, I am an artist, at least I would like to think so. I wanted to be an artist when I grew up.

As a child, I loved art. I grew up in the small village town of Brooklyn, New York, and created mosaics of graffiti art that colored the five boroughs of New York, and appeared vividly on trains. Acceptance to the prestigious Art and Design High School in New York City—was a testament to my early artistic talent and the institution's high regard for my cherished art portfolio. My father, however, would not let me enroll. "You will never make money as an artist," he said. He insisted, instead, that I attend Brooklyn Technical High School, a specialized science and engineering school requiring an entrance exam for admission. In retrospect, perhaps my father helped me make the right decision. Ultimately, I became a doctor and surgeon. However, I still love art, and *The Art of Human Care* is now my life's work.

THE GENESIS OF THE ART OF HUMAN CARE

In surgery, we say the natural course of one's disease is abruptly altered by the application of the cold hard steel of our scalpel. We induce trauma to change one's life, ideally for the better. Ultimately, it was as an undergrad, where a near-death experience and traumatic tragedy would set in motion a series of events destined to alter the course of my life. As a pre-med in college, I interviewed at Johns Hopkins Medical School under an early decision program. I was beyond excited. After my interview, I knew I was destined to become a doctor. I returned to my small college in upstate Plattsburgh, New York, to await the official news of my acceptance. Over the ensuing days, I became very ill with fever, chills, and the worst headache and neck pain of my life. I visited our college infirmary, was diagnosed (incorrectly) with gastroenteritis, prescribed penicillin tablets, and instructed to stay in bed and drink plenty of fluids. On a Friday night, alone in my room, and unable to call for help, two fraternity brothers, worried about me, entered my dorm room.

When they found me, I was lethargic and barely responsive. My friends rushed me to the Emergency Room at our local hospital. I remember sternal rubs, being told to hold still because a needle was going into my back and recall bright lights and masked people hovering over me. The doctor informed me I had a severe infection and could die. I was a patient. Many people experience being patients in their life, but not really. You are indeed a patient when you are stripped of your clothes, wear the hospital issued gown in humiliation, can no longer do things for yourself, and don't know what is going on. That happened to me. I did not understand what was happening to me. I was uncertain, anxious, scared, and thought I was going to die.

Fortunately, my healing mind took over and did what medicine alone could not have done. I had a positive outlook on my future, engendered by my recent interview for medical school, and a spirited soul that believed I was destined to become a healer. After all, I interviewed at Johns Hopkins and was determined not to let anything take me out. The process helped me to appreciate the power of thought, the mind, and how a positive, optimistic vision of one's future purpose could impact your health. It was the *ultimate* live-saving strategy.

FINDING PURPOSE

The truth about a near-death experience is that you are presented with two realities. First is the reality that you have just been given a second chance at life. Second is to appreciate and find the answer to a simple question with great urgency: why am I still alive? Contracting a lethal bacterial meningitis infection as a college junior, and delay in my diagnosis, delivered an otherwise fit, healthy, and an invincible young man to the intensive care unit with a tube in every orifice of my body. Only after emerging from my ordeal, did I learn the experts expected me to die. The odds were against me. Yet, I didn't die—I *exceeded* expectations. Since that fateful time in undergrad, the natural course of my life was abruptly altered. I've spent my life reconciling two realities. I was given a second chance at life, and there must be a reason why. Ultimately, I would learn Johns Hopkins would not accept me to medical school as I had hoped.

Although many years have passed since my near-death ordeal, I still remember the lessons learned about human care that being a patient taught me. My experience taught me about *empathy*, and what it feels like to be a patient. The average physician may have 80,000-100,000 patient encounters over a typical career. Thus, there are potentially 100,000 similar stories that patients like mine could share of the impact their healthcare encounter had on their life. Not all battles will be as involved as mine. However, in my career, I realize the work we do in healthcare engenders an incredible power and a gift to impact and affect the lives of others in a significant way and consequently change the world.

MAKING IT PERSONAL

I am a healer. On numerous occasions in life, including after learning the disappointing news from Johns Hopkins, I tried to run away from this fact. I also reflected with some regret on my abandoned aspiration to be an artist. In the process, an epiphany emerged. The art of healing through surgery is my singular purpose, and the reason I believe I'm here. To be a healer is the reason I survived death. I mean that in a physical, spiritual, and emotional way. My work in heart and lung transplantation exposes me repeatedly in a visceral way to the fragility of life and the physical reality of death. The reward and miracle of life that transplant brings to a desperately-ill recipient restores my optimism in the ethereal with every case. My highest satisfaction and joy come from helping others – through surgery, through inspiring, and through sharing a challenge or triumph I've overcome in my personal life – that aligns with another individual's story to offer hope for the possible.

The Art of Human Care is my prescription for the problem of sick-care focus, over health and wellness and the remedy for our inherent dissatisfaction with healthcare. Many people are not really feeling better when they engage with our healthcare system, and few discover they have a purpose. However, with an identified purpose, an individual can come alive and feel invigorated even with a terminal illness. I have seen it. I've seen people go from knocking on death's door to turn their life around and live a life full of passion and vigor with a purpose. Achieving health is our real goal, and it does not have to cost a lot. One does not have to cure to heal. Many people get their sick care at the hospital. However, there is seldom healing of the whole body and the individual in a hospital. True healing and subjective well-being come from someplace else. Typically, health and well-being come from a patient's support system of friends, family, community, church, or other places, not a healthcare system.

POWER IN PARTNERSHIPS

To achieve health through human care, I would argue, a necessary connection is needed beyond the hospital. We all need a purpose. With a purpose comes renewed life. For a patient, purpose transcends anything we, as providers, can give them in the hospital. A study of the ancient models of healing reveals healers *really* healed. Healers studied the whole body and appreciated the totality of an individual's relationships, existence, and experiences. The healers would note what was contributing to a patient's ill health, and observe when the body was out of balance. Today, despite our sophisticated diagnostics, our assessment of a patient's purpose is performed only in a cursory way. In this context, how much information is obtained in our traditional settings? How much will most patients reveal in a hurried office visit, the fleeting moment during hospital inpatient rounds, or in the bustling pace of an emergency room? To appreciate a patient's challenges in a meaningful way, let alone understand the patient's purpose, and address their needs, a different approach is needed. A *partnership* must be formed. This type of care rarely happens in our current settings. Yet, critical insight into a patient's purpose, and delivery of personalized human care, absolutely impact a person's health.

The Art of Human Care aims to change the world. Like the surgical example of cold hard steel altering the natural course of one's disease and problems, the art of human care alters the natural course of healthcare as we know it today. To inspire all those that care for humans, I thought critically about what it means to heal and present through the art of human care, a creative vision of how to change the world through healing. We need to promote health through purpose, personalization, and partnership. For with health, wisdom reveals itself, art becomes manifest, we have the strength to fight life's challenges, our wealth becomes useful, we may apply our intelligence and positively change the world.

The practice of human care represents the totality of my career in medicine. Human care combines the healing power of art, science, and inspiration delivered to all those that care for humans to create an evolving work. The singular aim of the art of human care is to heal individuals, promote health, and positively change the world. My experience as a surgeon, and aspiring artist confirms art is not merely an escape from work; instead, art is necessary to provide energy and inspiration to do *the work of healing* even better. Thus, art helps make the work of healing better. I've observed the positive effect on patients during healing arts exhibits. I suspect it is also the reason why art is ubiquitous on hospital walls, a sculpture is displayed, and music often fills the air in our places of healing and health. Art heals and indeed is a gift for the heart. Like my daughter the artist admonishes, without 'art' the heart is *just* "eh."

About Dr. Hassan A. Tetteh

Dr. Hassan A. Tetteh is a US Navy Captain and Associate Professor of Surgery at the Uniformed Services University of the Health Sciences and adjunct faculty at Howard University College of Medicine. He was a Robert Wood Johnson Health Policy Fellow from 2012-13, assigned to the US Congress, Congressional Budget Office, (CBO). Currently, Dr.Tetteh is a Thoracic Surgeon for MedStar Health and Walter Reed National Military Medical Center. He leads a Specialized Thoracic Adapted Recovery (STAR) Team, in Washington, DC, and his research in thoracic transplantation aims to expand heart and lung recovery and save lives.

A native of Brooklyn, New York, Hassan A. Tetteh received his BS from State University of New York (SUNY) at Plattsburgh, his MD from SUNY Downstate Medical Center, his MPA from Harvard's Kennedy School of Government, his MBA from Johns Hopkins University Carey Business School, and his MS in National Security Strategy with a concentration in Artificial Intelligence from the National War College. He completed his thoracic surgery fellowship at the University of Minnesota and advanced cardiac surgery fellowship at Harvard Medical School's Brigham and Women's Hospital in Boston.

Dr. Hassan A. Tetteh is founder and principal of Tetteh Consulting Group, a best-selling author of four books including *Gifts of the Heart, Star Patrol, The Art of Human Care*, and *Seven Pillars of Life*. He is board certified in thoracic surgery, general surgery, clinical informatics, and healthcare management, and is a Fellow of the American College of Surgeons and Fellow of the American College of Healthcare Executives.

Dr. Tetteh received the Alley Sheridan Award by the Thoracic Surgery Foundation for Research and Education, was named a TEDMED Front Line Scholar, and is a TEDx speaker. He's an alumnus of the Harvard Medical School Writers' Workshop and Yale Writers' Conference, and lives near Washington, D.C. with his wife, son, and daughter.

CHAPTER 3

STAY IN YOUR LANE

BY ERIC ZWIGART

If you want to grow your career or business,
then STAY IN YOUR LANE!!!
~ Eric Zwigart

Hello, a short introduction to who I am and what I think is a great one-line strategy to grow your career or Business. Given our time and chapter size, I will try to be as focused as possible!! My name is Eric Zwigart and I'm the CEO and Owner of RPP Products Company, Inc. Just 11 years ago, I was a 2-man operation working out of my house! Now I have 100+ employees operating in five states with gross sales over 125 million dollars per year.

In 2018, I won the Best of the Best Entrepreneurial Spirit Award. It's an award that goes to the Best Entrepreneur in the Inland Empire located in Southern CA. There were 229 companies/ entrepreneurs that competed, and I/we won the best in our business segment as well as overall "Best of the Best."

My company is an Automotive fluid distribution and manufacturing company. Which means we produce and sell Oils, ATF, Coolants, Additives, Aerosols. Well...... basically anything that is liquid that goes in or on a car!☺ We have two main brands we manufacturer ourselves: Race Pro and Premier. It is likely that you have or will see our products if you investigate your local C-Stores Automotive section or Grocery Auto section. Buy something please! Just kidding, only if you need it! At the very least you can say… "I read that guy's book!"

Back to the reason I want to mention the above growth is not to pump myself up or boast, but to show you that incredible growth of your career or business can be accomplished if you can remember to STAY IN YOUR LANE (SIYL).

Let's start with where or how I developed this phrase for myself and then how you can apply it. I found the concept in a business program/book from Michael Gerber called E-Myth. I was able to grab his concept and strategy and ran with it. BTW, I highly recommend if you are a new business owner or executive to either grab the E-Myth book or really any relevant business strategy consultant book and spend the time mapping out how you can break down your business or career. This is a great way to start learning how to best STAY IN YOUR LANE. There are tons of business strategies out there to help you, but the key is to be consistent and have faith in the strategy that you have chosen, provided it was built on a sound business or service need.

What does STAY IN YOUR LANE mean or refer to? It refers to a concept I often find myself saying to employees and myself more and more every day. It means that you have skills and a personality that makes you exceptional in many ways. However, you also have skills and personality that are sometimes a weakness or may hold you back. STAY IN YOUR LANE means focus on your own personal exceptional skills in your business or career and it will take you farther faster than trying to do everything well and going on overload. One of my biggest strengths and weaknesses in life and business is being Type A and super hyperactive. I am always wanting to do all things and wanting to do them right now. This trait helps me and motivates me to be productive, helps get things done, and helps others get projects going that they might have not wanted to get going. However, this trait hurts me at times because maybe myself or my business need a break to recover from the last round of projects, visions or entrepreneurial ideas I may have had. It relates to a simple true principle and saying, "you can do anything but not everything."

I use this term STAY IN YOUR LANE because as a business owner, I found that before you know it, by starting a company I created a job for myself but not freedom. You may ask what does that mean? Well I was tied to my job/company because I found myself constantly getting involved in every aspect of the business constantly. To this day it is a hard habit to break. However, you must remind yourself to SIYL. When you get too far down in the weeds, you can't see the forest through the trees. As a business owner or executive, you must remember that you can be some things to some people but not everything to everybody. Therefore, SIYL is also a reminder phrase for that.

Let's get into how this SIYL concept can help you right now:

1. DELEGATE OR STAGNATE
(Identify yourself and your team traits.)

In order to grow in your career or business ownership you must learn to delegate. The E-Myth book mentioned above categorizes people's personal traits and people themselves into 3 categories:

- *The Entrepreneur*
- *The Manager*
- *The Technician*

Which one are you? Or better put, which one are you the most dominant in….

Although we all have one of the three (3) traits below that is most dominant, we also have some of the other two traits that are there as well. So, you can define what a person is by one of the three traits while still knowing they possess and can use the other two as well. A good question to ask is: When it is the right time to use these traits? Here are my common examples of what these traits mean:

I. _The Entrepreneur._ This personal trait or person is the visionary and the strategy piece in everyone or its who you most identify with. This is the driver to make things move forward and change. Usually a business owner or Executive has more dominance of this trait than the other two. Hence, this is where the STAY IN YOUR LANE concept becomes more important.

II. _The Manager._ This personal trait or person is comfortable doing a little strategy but is good at organizing and making policies and procedures for The Technician to follow. Also, is generally good at managing but doesn't necessarily have the vision to move the business forward. They may be happy just staying busy at the current level of business you have.

III. _The Technician._ This personal trait or person is normally happy just doing their day-to-day tasks and going home. They enjoy busy work, and at some point, may be able to open and graduate to higher roles, but they move the dirt so to speak.

Understand and know that every employee or business owner in the business cycle has gone through all three roles or traits above at one time. However, its usually the business owner or executive that graduates because of the vision or strategy they possess to move things along. Hence, in that graduation, you must learn that if you are an executive or business owner you need to STAY IN YOUR LANE. Ask yourself the question: Out of the three traits above, what am I best or dominant at? If you are an Executive or Business Owner, the answer most likely is _The Entrepreneur._ That is most likely because you came up with the idea of how to work through towards being promoted in your company, or it's because you had a vision and an idea for a business, and you made it to this point. Here is a quick example using myself:

38

I'm an Entrepreneur through and through. Although, through the various business cycles I needed to be *The Manager* or *The Technician* at times, but who I really am is a guy that focuses on vision and strategy to grow my businesses and help people achieve and exceed their goals.

Now what? You need to use your teams help. Do you have employees under you? If so, define them and give them direction to accomplish your vision.

Grow your visions and strategies through your network of mangers and technicians below you. DON'T TRY TO BE INVOLVED IN EVERTYHING…. STAY IN YOUR LANE! YOU'RE AN ENTREPRENEUR! SO BE ONE!

2. GROW YOUR VISION AND IDEAS THROUGH YOUR PERSONNEL

a. If you are an Executive or Business Owner, use your team to help you reach your goals. Elevate all your people up all the way down to the bottom manager and technician you have.

b. You must evaluate which dominant trait each of your team members possess and then put them in a position to succeed. You need to have discussions about these three traits and that person's own natural abilities. After that you can position people to understand what lane they need to stay in.

(i). Breakdown your team and constantly keep that machine of people below you fed with direction to move your Vision and Strategies along.

(ii). Generals/Managers can't be in the trenches on the battlefield or they will lose the overall perspective to win the war. You are the General in your current business scenario. Therefore, you need to keep your managers on target with direction and your technicians loaded with work and positive incentives to start crushing their goals which will in turn crush your goals!

(iii). Position reports. Go ahead and have all your people write up their own job descriptions and send them to you. After that modify them accordingly have a meeting to discuss and then have that person sign that document. It makes their direction and responsibilities very clear to both sides.

c. Grow your team appropriately. Add pieces (people) if they are needed to make the next goal or needed to enhance the productivity of the team you have under you. Add people as necessary only if it makes sense that you can hit your next goal faster. Do the ROI and evaluate the business on a case-by-case basis. If by adding someone and if it checks out financially, do it!

d. Get your company or team moving into an organizational chart that looks like a pyramid. You are on top and you want fewer managers than technicians. You want to be able to have the managers map out redundant tasks to the technicians and drive them to meet their goals. The managers will assist. However, you don't want your managers being technicians more than 50% of their time, otherwise they just become high-paid technicians. Trust me, I get this a lot. To this day we all work on trying to get the managers out of the weeds at times to be able to spend more time in strategy and bigger picture growth. I must tell them all and myself truthfully STAY IN YOUR LANE!!!

3. STAY IN YOUR LANE RECAP

a. Identify what type of person your traits show that you are.

    (i). The Entrepreneur
    (ii). The Manger
    (iii). The Technician

b. If you are mostly the Entrepreneur/Manager which, chances are you are… since you're reading this book… listen to this and understand you must focus on being a good Entrepreneur and that means STAY IN YOUR LANE and delegate work to your team, organization or company. I know it's hard, but do it and watch the work and "machine" begin to run itself without your assistance all the time.

c. I have added a chart or breakdown which I consider ideal for the positions in my company including myself following this recap.

4. THE PERFECT SCENARIOS

OWNER/CEO

Ideally how I would spend my work time (THE ENTREPRENEUR)

- 50%: The Entrepreneur – On the vision, direction and strategy of the business and where it's going.

- 40%: The Manager – Talking to my President, VPs, and staff on my ideas and how I can help them.

- 10%: The Technician – Working on the actual implementation of the vision and its details, policies, procedures, etc. so that they can work moving forward without continually going back to work on them. Always try to automate everything you come across so that you are not having to do the same thing over and over if it can be automated.

MANAGERS

Ideally how they would spend their work time (THE MANAGERS/VPs)

- 25%: The Entrepreneur – On the vision, direction and strategy of the business and where it's going. Discussing things with upper management and preparing to get our team achieving those goals.

- 50%: The Manager – Talking to my technicians and getting them the direction and implementations of policies and procedures to try and automate their jobs better. Keep them on point to meet the team's goals.

- 25%: The Technician – Being a manager you must get in the weeds some but not all the time. Remember Entrepreneurs and Mangers must try to see the forest through the trees.

TECHNICIANS

Ideally how they would spend their work time. (THE TECHNICIANS) (Also, most cost-effective mover of dirt so to speak....)

- 10%: The Entrepreneur – They listen to management direction give possible feedback and then implement what needs done.

- 10%: The Manager – The technician needs to focus on just moving the needle forward on their work and must focus on their tasks not managing other people.

- 80%: The Technician – Moving dirt... Getting work done. Constantly doing the job description/ job agreement they have been given. Doing all the redundant/ repetitive tasks of the company and needing minimal help to do so. When tasks are finished help another person on their team.

In closing, hopefully you understand the concept and the one-line strategy of STAY IN YOUR LANE. Again, one last time do what you do best and let your team do what they do best!

EVERYONE TRY TO STAY IN YOUR LANE!

About Eric

Eric Zwigart was born in 1975 in Pittsburgh, PA, but he essentially grew up in PA, AZ and CA. As a child, Eric was the youngest of two boys (SZ). Growing up in those three states for his first 18 years provided him a lot of different life experiences. It also broadened his perspective of living styles, diversity, and gave him a well-rounded outlook of how and where he wanted to end up in life. In 1992, Eric and his mother Joann Zwigart decided PA was the best place for him to eventually attend college, so he spent his Senior Year of High School attending Chartiers Valley H.S. and graduated in 1993.

Eric Zwigart graduated from California University of PA in 1998 with a bachelor's degree in Business Management. While attending college, Eric joined the United State Marine Corps as a Military Police Officer reservist from 1995-2001. After graduating from college and finishing his time in the USMC Reserves, Eric started working for his father, Anthony Zwigart's Oil company in Southern California, Chalet Products Company. As Sales Manager with Chalet Products Company, Eric was able to grow the wholesale sales segment from $200k per year into $2.5M per year within 1 year (10x in 1 year). This continued success then lead to an eventual VP of Sales position, leading the entire company's sales responsibilities. After being with the company for eight years, Chalet was sold to Amalie Oil Company. At that point, Eric decided to start his own company.

In March 2006, Eric took the huge leap of faith in business and started RPP Products, Inc. Amazingly, starting in 2006 as a 1-man operation, RPP Products has rapidly grown into a $125+M company with 100+ employees, and is the leader in Convenience Retail, Grocery, Wholesale and other market segments. RPP provides Private Label, and other logistics and distribution solutions to both retailers and suppliers for the Automotive category, RPP currently serves its customer base from four locations with number five coming soon.

Proudly, in 2018 Eric Zwigart was nominated for the So-Cal Spirit of Entrepreneur awards. These awards are given to the most deserving companies and owners that embrace Entrepreneurship in Southern CA Inland Empire. There were 229 nominees and Eric won "the Oscar" award of them all: **"The 2018 Best of Best 2018 Spirit of the Entrepreneur."** (https://spiritawardsie.com/)

To this day Eric Z continues to drive his visions and strategies to his team in order to keep growing his companies at an ever-forward moving pace. His personal, business and life motto is: "Don't look into the rear-view mirror while driving for too long…. you will no doubt eventually crash !!!"

You can contact Eric at:
- ezstrategies@rppproducts.com or at www.rppproducts.com

CHAPTER 4

BELIEF, TRUST... FAITH = SUCCESS

BY ADREINA ADAMS

I was blessed to have started working in a professional environment at the age of fourteen. There was good furniture, water coolers or fountains, lockers, bulletin boards, and adequate supplies like pens and pencils.

When I started my adult career at eighteen, it was quite different. We had no lockers, bulletin boards, supplies, or respect. Other young women and I were subjected to sexual harassment and retaliation. Some of the older male supervisors would ask us to sit on their laps, try to rub our shoulders, or ask us out on dates. Those of us who refused were given the worst assignments and not allowed to have weekends or holidays off.

I didn't have names for the behavior or treatment at the time, but I knew that it was wrong. I understood that union dues were being withheld from my pay but had no idea what a union was or what they did, so I inquired as to what it was.

Once I learned the purpose and power of a union, I became actively involved, eventually taking on a leadership role. As a result, the unfair behavior from management ceased, we were given fairly rotated schedules, and one of my members was even awarded fifteen thousand dollars in back-pay because of unfair treatment. I proudly continued my union work there for many years.

Eventually, I changed my career path and began working for the State of New York as a parole officer. This didn't mean I would be hanging up my union reins, however.

When I went to the State, I was shocked by the unacceptable working conditions. There were no lockers, bulletin boards, or supplies. We were expected to handle unmanageable numbers of caseloads using broken furniture, insufficient and inadequate equipment, and unreliable, unsafe vehicles. My colleagues and I were given a two-door jeep with no air conditioning to conduct delinquency work. Imagine riding around the streets of New York with a bulletproof vest on in the summertime, with no air conditioning. It was miserable work.

The agency provided an unacceptable, unsupportive, and unprofessional work environment, but the agency had high expectations and demands of us. I felt compelled to continue my union work.

I hold the **belief** that if you are not part of the solution, then you are part of the problem, so once established in the union, I embarked on a campaign to improve the working conditions. I participated in press conferences, legislative hearings, lobbying, and demonstrations. I appeared on radio, newspaper, and television. I worked with other union leaders to motivate, inspire, and guide the members to advocate for themselves. It was a long, protracted campaign that ultimately resulted in new vehicles, new furniture, lockers, equipment and supplies, reduced caseloads, a reduction of redundant paperwork, and more staff to help handle it.

I consider myself a faithful servant and have dedicated the last 38 years to serving others. As a faithful servant, I have held many professional positions. The only position that spans the entire 38 years is my role as a union leader.

As a union leader, I challenged the status quo in both the union and management. As a result of my staunch advocacy, thousands of employee's work environments improved. They saw an increase in their income, were finally treated with dignity and respect, provided with policy and procedures that were adhered to, and were given a voice in the workplace.

These changes occurred over the course of years and were the result of **faith** that systemic change could occur in spite of what appeared to be insurmountable challenges, obstacles, and opposition.

> *I have always chosen to do <u>What</u> I can, <u>Where</u> I am,*
> *with <u>What</u> I have, to make things better.*

I have never been someone to chase money, prestige, or titles. My fulfillment came from doing what I believed was God's work – to make and leave things better than I found them. I was blessed to be able to do exactly that during the last 21 years as a parole officer. My role was to help people gain confidence, have faith, dream, develop life plans, increase their incomes, get or change jobs, develop and maintain healthy relationships and transform. This was the most wonderful aspect of my job... along with my union work, I was able to fulfill my purpose in life.

Unfortunately, there were some who didn't appreciate my union leadership, and I was subjected to retaliation. I was brought up on false charges of harassment and was disciplined because agency representatives engaged in witness tampering, interference, and sabotage.

I was given a punishment that was unprecedented – never given to anyone prior or since – of a permanent assignment to the

Brooklyn Bureau, covering the largest, most violent precinct in NYC. I believe that they thought that I would leave the agency.

My **faith** let me know that I could handle it and make it work. I was put here for a reason, by a *much higher authority* than anyone at the agency, and *I would not let HIM down*.

In Brooklyn, I was ostracized and made to do the majority of my fieldwork alone – because I wasn't given an office partner. No office partner meant I had no one to rely on, and if anyone attempted to be supportive, they were subjected to retaliation. I went into some of the most dangerous buildings and projects alone, with no one to rely on. However, I partnered with God, so who else did I really need?

The retaliation and hostile work environment continued and intensified. I had to be hyper-vigilant and on guard with everything that I did. My written reports would disappear off my desk, and I had to review for accuracy if I went to court, because often, they would be changed. My intuition led me to print everything out and keeping it on me at all times, for my protection.

In spite of being ostracized, not only did I stay at the agency, but I also continued my work as a union leader.

I began to address the unprofessional and unsanitary conditions of the Brooklyn office. We were often forced to work much later hours than scheduled and lacked many basic items like toilet paper, paper towels, and soap in the bathrooms. It might sound insignificant, but to me, if we were not worthy of such basic things, then certainly we weren't worthy of more critical things like safe vehicles, equipment, etc.

The job of a parole officer is high stress, high demand, and multi-faceted – wearing many hats. We are law enforcement officers and act as social workers. We conduct our own urinalyses, investigations, delinquency work, interviews, and represent the agency against attorneys at delinquency hearings, to name a few. It was an honor and privilege to be able to do the work and provide assistance to people who were formerly incarcerated to be able to reintegrate them back into the community successfully, but our primary job was to stay safe and keep everyone else safe.

It is my belief that every person in an organization is entitled to be treated with respect, and given the proper tools, equipment, training, and resources to do their jobs.

There came a point where the stress of doing my job, coupled with the non-stop retaliation, became too much. I lost weight, my hair started falling out, and I was often sick. I had worked enough years to be eligible for retirement but had not reached the required age, so I settled for a leave of absence to take time to heal. While out on sick leave, I received a call from a colleague that a notice of discipline (NOD) was issued for me. Once again, the charges were false, and I was fed up.

I felt that once again I was being bullied, dehumanized, devalued, and rendered *persona non grata*. I was infuriated that the administration could be so insensitive and petty enough to kick a person when they are down, and I headed back to work, determined to fight the NOD.

I embarked on a gloves-off defense, choosing not to rely solely on the guidance of my representative. I had to do extensive research, computer review and in-depth analysis to challenge the allegations that I had not done my work, but the proper evidence was obtained, and one by one, their false charges were challenged and crumbled.

During the process, I did a LOT of praying and remained steadfast in the **faith** that God would order my footsteps and lead me to a successful outcome, and that's just what He did.

I had boxes of documents at home, in no particular order, and

God would direct me to the right box when I needed to find a document to refute, substantiate, or justify various statements, documents, assertions or untruths.

At one point, my representative tried to convince me to take the letter of reprimand that they offered because 'you never know what the arbitrator will rule.' I had done nothing wrong, though, and my faith would not allow me to do settle. My assertion is that living in this world is a gamble. We never know what is going to happen. Faith allows us to prepare for another day.

Going into dangerous buildings and apartments by myself was a risk, but my faith in God kept me safe and allowed me to do my job, lifting up those who needed my help. My faith would not waver when faced with this trial.

I knew that if someone finds you guilty it does not mean that the findings are accurate. If you bargain, it is difficult to assert your innocence. My faith said I should proceed, because I would win. No doubts. Just do exactly as I am directed by God and I would win. I did not let anyone persuade me to do something that was contrary to what God was directing me to do. The outcome? I won.

Not long after, I decided to run for the position of Vice President of my union. It was a long shot, but I had faith that I could win. In spite of the many challenges and obstacles, I won.

In all things, **faith** is fundamental. **Faith** is the cornerstone for success. The successful realization of a dream or vision is born of faith. *Without faith there is failure.* **Faith** creates a synergistic force that provides motivation, excitement, relentless pursuit and passion that enables action to be taken and followed through to its successful outcome.

For truly I tell you, if you have faith as small as a mustard seed
you can say to this mountain, 'Move from here to there'
and it will move. Nothing will be impossible for you.
~ Mathew 17:20

As Vice President of the union, I have helped members to increase their income, get good contracts, get needed supplies, equipment, and improve their working conditions and environments. None of my achievements or success would have been possible without **faith**.

Faith helped me to be dogmatic, never give up in spite of what appeared to be insurmountable obstacles and challenges. When there are naysayers, when it appears that you can't or won't succeed and you want to give up, **faith** is the fuel that lets you know that it's not **IF** you will succeed, but **WHEN** you will succeed. **Faith** is the wind beneath my wings. **Faith** makes the impossible possible.

Faith fosters creativity and ingenuity. **Faith** provides comfort when there are disappointments. **Faith** lets you know that you will rise again.

Without **faith** you can't have courage. **Faith** is where miracles are born, blossom and grow.

Faith is taking the first step even when you don't
see the whole staircase.
~ Dr. Martin Luther King

About Adreina

As a coach, consultant and speaker for 39 years, Adreina Adams has helped thousands of people to become motivated, have confidence, excel in their careers, increase their income, pursue their dreams and achieve success.

A few of the speaking engagements that she has participated in were at the American Federation of Teachers, Public Employees Federation, Black and Hispanic Legislative Caucus weekend, SOMOS Legislative weekend and the Murphy Institute.

For 34 years, Adreina Adams has worked as a union leader and aggressive fighter against injustice. She has worked as a parole officer for 21 years and has worked as a mediator-arbitrator.

An outspoken union leader, Adreina has testified at legislative hearings, met independently with legislators to draft bills, spoken at press conferences, workshops, rallies, and demonstrations, and been interviewed by radio, TV and newspapers – which resulted in a variety of systematic improvements.

As Vice President of the Public Employees Federation, she modernized the union by being the catalyst for the creation of a data management system and systemic operational improvements, both of which have led to optimum success.

Adreina Adams earned her BPS degree from the College for Human Services. Adreina received certification in Interpersonal Behavior and Conflict Resolution from the Cornell University School of Industrial & Labor Relations, earned certification in Basic Union Peer Counseling from the NYC Central Labor Council, is a Certified Coach and a Cornell ILR graduate.

CHAPTER 5

SPECIALIZED KNOWLEDGE: THE CELEBRITY BRANDING SECRET OF SUCCESS

BY NICK NANTON AND JW DICKS

Napoleon Hill calls "specialized knowledge" the fourth step to riches in his pioneering self-help book, *Think and Grow Rich*.

For anyone who wants to establish their own Celebrity Brand, however, specialized knowledge is actually THE key to success and the strategy we're going to discuss in this chapter.

At our Agency, we know what makes our clients special and stand out from the rest is their specialized knowledge. The trick is to make their potential leads (and the general public) aware of what they have to offer – and how it can improve the lives of those who hire them.

In this chapter, we're going to pull back the curtain and let you in on some of the "magic" behind our biggest Celebrity Branding® secrets. We'll discuss the power of specialized knowledge, why it's an important success strategy and how to promote it in credible and impactful ways that lead to a new level of success.

In the words of Napoleon Hill himself, *"There are two kinds of knowledge. One is general, the other is specialized. General knowledge...is of but little use in the accumulation of money.... the accumulation of great fortunes calls for POWER, and power is acquired through highly organized and intelligently-directed specialized knowledge."*

Sounds good to us!

THE LASTING VALUE OF SPECIALIZED KNOWLEDGE

None of us can be experts on everything. Now, we've certainly met people who actually did know a little bit about everything. They can be very interesting to talk to. But, when you actually need some real in-depth advice for a specific concern, you need more than a stimulating conversation. You need expertise – the expertise that comes from *specialized knowledge.*

Think about it. When you have a tax problem, are you just going to listen to your cousin who got audited six years ago and thinks he knows everything about the IRS? Or are you going to listen to a tax attorney who keeps current with all the latest legislation?

When you have a specific pain, are you going to listen to your friend who played college basketball about what he learned when he pulled a hamstring – or are you going to go to a specialist whose practice involves the area of your body that's currently plaguing you?

When there's something important going on in your life that affects your business, your finances, your health or even your relationship, you want to go beyond casual talk with people who have had limited experience in your "area of pain." You want to talk to someone who knows everything there is to know about the specific concern you need addressed. You want to see THE expert in solving the problem you have.

That's why specialized knowledge is so valuable. As Napoleon Hill makes clear in his chapter about specialized knowledge, it *always* has a value to those who, at the time, desperately need it. Even when it comes to the act of making money, Hill writes, "Before you can be sure of your ability to transmute DESIRE into its monetary equivalent, you will require SPECIALIZED KNOWLEDGE of the service, merchandise or profession which you intend to offer in return for fortune."

But, as Hill also makes clear, many do, in fact, have vast amounts of specialized knowledge – and yet they still don't profit greatly from it. In his words, "The faculties of the great universities possess, in the aggregate, practically every form of general knowledge known to civilization. *Most of the professors have but little or no money.*"

Those italics are courtesy of Hill, not us! While we respect men of learning, we also believe they should be able to profit from that learning. Specialized knowledge can be, to use Hill's word, "transmuted" into healthy profit.

Let's talk about how you can make that happen.

MARKETING SPECIALIZED KNOWLEDGE

So, what's the difference between a successful businessperson and a doctor, attorney or other professional who has the kind of specialized knowledge people need on a regular basis?

Simple. The businessperson's specialized knowledge usually has to do with *how to make money*. The focus is completely on the bottom line – whereas the professional is usually focused on whatever his or her area of expertise is all about. The doctor or lawyer, for example, spends many extra years beyond the standard four years of college learning his or her profession; the typical entrepreneur, by contrast, could easily be a high school drop-out (and, as a matter of fact, many of our biggest titans of industry over the years never got their high school diploma).

Hill addresses this point by recounting the story of Ford Motors founder Henry Ford, who was one of those super successful men who had little formal education. Ford was embroiled in a lawsuit and was being challenged by a group of lawyers who were out to prove that he was not too smart. They began peppering him with simple history questions that any schoolboy might know – the problem was, Ford didn't spend a whole lot of time being a schoolboy.

Fed up with the taunting, Ford finally replied, "If I should really WANT to answer the foolish question you have just asked, let me remind you that I have a row of electric push-buttons on my desk, and, by pushing the right button, I can summon to my aid men who can answer ANY question I desire to ask...WHY should I clutter my mind...when I have men around me who can supply any knowledge I require?"

This reflects a very traditional view of specialized knowledge - the "big fish" like Ford made all the money and simply paid for that kind of expertise when they needed it.

But why shouldn't those with specialized knowledge be big fish too?

They worked hard to obtain their knowledge and experience – shouldn't that entitle them to more?

ENTER THE CELEBRITY EXPERT®

That's why we enjoy elevating those with their own unique specialized knowledge to a new position in their industry – and in the public's eyes. The Celebrity Expert® is famous and successful precisely because he or she has a certain kind of specialized knowledge that's in demand. People seek out Celebrity Experts®, instead of vice-versa, simply because their reputations precede them.

Think of people like Dr. Oz and Dr. Phil – they're the ultimate in Celebrity Experts®, and, of course, they really don't have to go knocking on anyone's doors – the public comes knocking on theirs. With all due respect to those two gentlemen, though, we have to say we're sure there are thousands of doctors out there who are just as qualified as them – just not as rich and famous.

Why? Because *millions* know who Dr. Oz and Dr. Phil are – while, in comparison, very few people know those other doctors. The fact of the matter is that the difference between Celebrity Experts® and their peers doesn't necessarily have anything to do with them being better at what they do – no, it's often just a question of *effective marketing of their positioning.*

This is the point where many professionals sigh and say they don't want to market themselves. They feel it somehow demeans them. They feel it should be enough to be able to excel at what they do – that alone should bring people in through their doors. Our experience is that's a very risky way to think. At best, unaided word of mouth takes years and years to build – and, at worst, someone who doesn't effectively market themselves never gets new clients to replace the old ones who either move on or pass away.

Frankly, with all the economic upheavals of recent years, everyone is looking for every possible advantage in the marketplace. That means if you're *not* marketing yourself, odds are your competitors *are* – and your potential clients or customers, not knowing any better, are going to end up going with the ones making the best case for themselves, i.e., the ones that are doing the best marketing, as opposed to you.

Imagine a lawyer finishing a difficult case – and choosing not to make a closing argument. What's the jury supposed to think? Well, that's kind of the point of a closing argument, isn't it? – to frame the case so the jury looks at it from your point of view. Without that kind of guidance, those twelve men and women are probably just going to latch on to what the opposing lawyer is saying.

Well, that's basically the situation in which professionals and entrepreneurs who refuse to market properly are putting themselves; they're not making a case for their specialized knowledge and those that might have hired them *never find out that they should.*

CELEBRITY EXPERTS® REQUIRE EXPERT MARKETING

Part of the reason professionals don't feel comfortable with marketing is that the word "marketing" immediately makes them think of the worst TV commercial they recently saw. Maybe it was a cheesy infomercial for the latest glued-together combination of metal and springs that's supposed to give you super-abs – or maybe it's some famous football player yelling at you from the TV about how to get your prostate in shape with his brand of vitamins.

We're the first to agree that this is not the way to market a Celebrity Expert®. No, the way to market a Celebrity Expert® is to take advantage of the most important thing he or she has to offer – which takes us right back to the subject of this chapter, *specialized knowledge.*

In other words, we're not suggesting they should be out there doing TV commercials where they wear cowboy hats and ride on elephants (don't laugh, a car dealer in California used to do that!)—and we're not discouraging it either....if it aligns with your brand. Instead, they should appear in *venues and in situations that fit their brand, offering their expertise.*

We do this through several media channels for our Celebrity Expert® clients. In this next section of the chapter, we're going to share some of the main ways we market them in a way that doesn't embarrass them (or us!) – and how you can easily take advantage of them yourself:

- **Newspapers and Magazines**
  It would be awesome to find yourself profiled in an article in a major periodical like *The Wall Street Journal, USA Today* and *Forbes*, right? Especially if that article focused on all the good stuff about you and featured quotes from you that demonstrated your specialized knowledge. Well, that's just what we do for our clients – and it's easy enough to do on your own in your community. There are always local newspapers and magazines that are hunting for good content; just provide it to them in the form of an interview or by writing an article on a subject that you're an expert on and that their readers will want to read about.

- **TV and Radio Shows**
  We produce many television and radio shows, such as our America's PremierExperts® programs, in which we feature our clients being interviewed about their work by media professionals. These shows air on ABC, NBC, CBS and FOX affiliates across the nation. For your part, there are always local "talking head" radio and TV talk shows that are anxious for guests who are interesting and have informative content to share. Look for topics that will work for them and you and contact them about a possible interview. And don't forget – you can even do your own podcast and put it up on iTunes!

- **Blogs and Articles**
  Online blogging (and article posting) still definitely makes an impact; we help our clients place their content on such popular sites as T*he Huffington Post* and *Fast Company.* You should consider blogging on your own site and also posting articles on other sites that accept your kind of content (always make sure you include a link back to your site when you do that).

- **Books**
  Nothing says "expert" more than showing a potential client a book authored by you. And it's not all that hard to pull off, even if time is at a premium in your schedule. There are a myriad of publishing options out there, as well as affordable ghostwriters who will actually help you complete the work. We're proud to say we've helped over 1,000 professionals become Best-Selling authors – and most of them are ecstatic that they're able to use that fact in their marketing to help boost their profile and their prestige with their clientele. Think about it, who would you rather hire, the Best-Selling author...or the other guy? Easy choice right!

- **Videos and Branded Films**
  Using online video is a giant industry that's getting even bigger with each passing year. Here are two important stats that prove it, according to a recent Content Marketing Institute (CMI) survey:

  - Over 85% of online users viewed video content in September 2012 alone.
  - About 46% of people are more apt to research a product or service after watching an online video about it.

Video and film are also great for showcasing your personality and establishing a personal connection to potential clients and customers: They bring an extra dimension to marketing that can be invaluable. This kind of content can be as simple as "How-To" videos on YouTube, featuring you talking directly to the camera about a subject in your area of expertise, or they can be fully-produced branded films that tell your story, as well as the story of your business or practice, so viewers understand what you're all about. We've produced many of these for clients, who have seen outstanding results from them. In all of the above marketing examples, you may notice there's not a lot of hard sell. We don't believe that's effective for most professionals and entrepreneurs. What we do believe is most effective, in terms of marketing, is for a

Celebrity Expert® to: (a) demonstrate they have a high level of specialized knowledge, and (b) provide a taste of that knowledge (with some personality infused) to give those exposed to the marketing some *value* from having seen it, making it a win-win. Whether you're an entrepreneur who's achieved a high degree of success or a professional who has worked hard to build your expertise to an outstanding level, you have specialized knowledge that will benefit others. When you use high-level marketing to successfully *convey* that specialized knowledge through your own words, you not only boost your recognition factor, but you also create *credibility* and the beginnings of a personal bond.

A Celebrity Expert® is someone who knows the value of their specialized knowledge and has successfully communicated it to the world. And there's no reason you can't join their ranks.

About Nick

An Emmy Award-Winning Director and Producer, Nick Nanton, Esq., produces media and branded content for top thought leaders and media personalities around the world.

Recognized as a leading expert on branding and storytelling, Nick has authored more than two dozen Best-Selling books (including *The Wall Street Journal* Best-Seller, *StorySelling*™) and produced and directed more than 50 documentaries, earning 11 Emmy Awards and 26 nominations. Nick speaks to audiences internationally on the topics of branding, entertainment, media, business and storytelling at major universities and events.

As the CEO of DNA Media, Nick oversees a portfolio of companies including: The Dicks + Nanton Agency (an international agency with more than 3,000 clients in 63 countries), Dicks + Nanton Productions, Ambitious.com and DNA Films. Nick is an award-winning director, producer and songwriter who has worked on everything from large scale events to television shows with the likes of Steve Forbes, Ivanka Trump, Sir Richard Branson, Larry King, Jack Nicklaus, Rudy Ruettiger (inspiration for the Hollywood Blockbuster, *RUDY*), Brian Tracy, Jack Canfield (*The Secret*, creator of the *Chicken Soup for the Soul*® Series), and many more.

Nick has been seen in *USA Today, The Wall Street Journal, Newsweek, BusinessWeek, Inc. Magazine, The New York Times, Entrepreneur*® *Magazine, Forbes* and *Fast Company*, and has appeared on ABC, NBC, CBS, and FOX television affiliates across the country, as well as on CNN, FOX News, CNBC, and MSNBC coast-to-coast.

Nick is a member of the Florida Bar, a member of The National Academy of Television Arts & Sciences (Home to the EMMYs), co-founder of The National Academy of Best-Selling Authors®, and serves on the Innovation Board of the XPRIZE Foundation, a non-profit organization dedicated to bringing about "radical breakthroughs for the benefit of humanity" through incentivized competition and best known for its Ansari XPRIZE—which incentivized the first private space flight and was the catalyst for Richard Branson's Virgin Galactic. He was a recipient of the Global Shield Humanitarian Award in Feb. 2019.

Nick also enjoys serving as an Elder at Orangewood Church, working with Young Life, Entrepreneurs International and rooting for the Florida Gators with his wife Kristina and their three children, Brock, Bowen and Addison.

Learn more at:
- www.NickNanton.com
- www.CelebrityBrandingAgency.com
- www.DNAmedia.com

About JW

JW Dicks, Esq., is the CEO of DN Agency, an Inc. 5000 Multimedia Company that represents over 3,000 clients in 63 countries.

He is a *Wall Street Journal* Best-Selling Author® who has authored or co-authored over 47 books, a 5-time Emmy® Award-winning Executive Producer and a Broadway Show Producer.

JW is an Ansari XPRIZE Innovation Board member, Chairman of the Board of the National Retirement Council™, Chairman of the Board of the National Academy of Best-Selling Authors®, Board Member of the National Association of Experts, Writers and Speakers®, and a Board Member of the International Academy of Film Makers®.

He has been quoted on business and financial topics in national media such as *USA Today, The Wall Street Journal, Newsweek, Forbes, CNBC.com*, and *Fortune Magazine Small Business.*

JW has co-authored books with legends like Jack Canfield, Brian Tracy, Tom Hopkins, Dr. Nido Qubein, Steve Forbes, Richard Branson, Michael Gerber, Dr. Ivan Misner, and Dan Kennedy.

JW has appeared and interviewed on business television shows airing on ABC, NBC, CBS, and FOX affiliates around the country and co-produces and syndicates a line of franchised business television shows such as *Success Today, Wall Street Today, Hollywood Live*, and *Profiles of Success.*

JW and his wife of 47 years, Linda, have two daughters, and four granddaughters. He is a sixth-generation Floridian and splits his time between his home in Orlando and his beach house on Florida's west coast.

CHAPTER 6

"SPRINGS OF CREATION"

BY DR. ANNA PAVLINA CHARALAMBOUS

This is not a 'success in business' chapter, this is a 'success in life' chapter. This is a story that I wish to spread all over the world to let people know that success in life starts by creating a healthy inner world, and that its creation is something we can choose.

"I know I wished my life to end, but God I didn't mean it."

These were the words that kept running in my mind when I managed to lay in my bed, after a nightmare ride in a tram and after being totally ridiculed in a central square of Amsterdam. I was sitting on a bench in the middle of the square crying – crying because I felt I was going crazy, crying because I felt I was going to die. People were looking at me, some laughing at me, not realizing I had taken drugs, or realizing it and thinking I was stupid to have taken them in public. I called some of my friends that were also visiting Amsterdam to come and help, but they did not realize the importance of what was going on. They didn't take what was happening too seriously you see, or maybe they didn't want to interrupt their joyful experience.

After a long time, I found myself in a taxi with my two hotel roommates who had totally 'lost it' and were hallucinating as well, due to the drugs we had taken together. I was scared that the taxi driver would take advantage of us as we were not in a position to react or to protect ourselves, but thankfully, we reached the hotel.

Just to take you back a few steps, what I have described was a result of being so unhappy with my life that I didn't want to continue living it. I didn't see a reason to live because I was experiencing sadness, anxiety and misery every day. I didn't want to be miserable anymore. I was in my second year of studies back in beautiful Canterbury in the U.K., studying to be a psychologist.

I was a super sociable young woman, and even though I was getting a lot of attention, I found it hard to truly connect with people. I found most of my interactions with other students to be shallow and found their interests of drinking, smoking, drugs, status, looks, and having random sex with random people not being aligned with who I was.

I cared about poetry, art, dancing and music. I cared about cultures, languages, love and spirituality. I felt I was too deep and too weird, and I just wanted to be like everyone else. I just wanted to be normal and to fit in. I thought I was too emotional, too sensitive and I blamed myself for being so different.

I wanted to belong, and I started doing everything I could to change. I was trying to be something I was not. You see, I wasn't aware of the secrets of life back then. Through this change, I lost me, I lost who I was and what I supported in life.

By suppressing myself, I started feeling very sad. I remember thinking that there was no point in living, thinking my life was worthless. Thus, I started acting in disrespectful ways towards my body – even if it felt very wrong.

I was doing all these things just to belong and to escape from all the negative feelings I was experiencing. I started drinking, even if it made me feel bad, just because everybody was doing it. I started smoking, even if I was the biggest antismoker, just because a new friend asked me to share the experience with her. Last but not least, I decided to take a trip to Amsterdam with a lot of University students that were regular weed users, even if my gut instinct was telling me that I should not go. I ignored it.

I also said I would try drugs while there, just because my friends were up for it – even though being without them was my personal desire.

One thing led to another, and during my Amsterdam visit, I had a whole piece of a 'space cake' without truly wanting to, without learning what having one would feel like first, without knowing what this could do to me. I did it just to have the experience, just because I was asked to share the fun. Me and my two roommates had it when we were in our hotel room and I consented to doing something of which I had no idea where it could lead.

The effect was not instant, we felt nothing right after we ate it, so we left the room to go out in busy Amsterdam. We took a tram and while we were riding it, it hit us… and it was a huge hit. We didn't realize that it was related to our 'space cake' ingestion at first.

We were young, we were inexperienced, we were naïve. I think none of us expected to feel this way, none of us expected the feeling of having no control to hit us in such an unprotected environment.

We lost control and we did not know when to get off the tram, who to call for help, or what to do in order to experience the "trip" in the most pleasant way possible. Unfortunately, I was the least lucky out of the three, because I ate a whole piece of space cake, when it is recommended to have just a bite or just a part of it. What I was experiencing was really intense, more intense than I could handle.

It was a scary ride, a very scary one, but we managed to reach our hotel after 2-3 hours, feeling lost and helpless.

A fellow University student managed to put us in a taxi, but he did not get in the taxi with us, for what reason I still don't know. When we reached the hotel, he was there waiting for us. He guided us to our room and stayed with us, trying to calm us down. He was a regular weed user, so he somehow knew that what we were going through was a bad trip.

I begged him and my two roommates to tell all my friends, family and relatives how much I loved them. This was my last request since I was convinced that my life was about to end. I felt that this was my last day on earth. I remember myself praying, letting God know that I didn't want my life to end anymore.

At the same time, I was too tired trying to fight this force taking over me.

After I laid on my bed, I decided to surrender to this feeling that was taking over my body, soul and mind. I was convinced that I was surrendering to death. I couldn't explain what I was feeling in any other way.

I asked God to forgive my sins and then I dived into the black abyss...

The next morning when I opened my eyes, I couldn't believe I was alive. I was alive and my life changed color. I wrote something on that next day that better describes what I went through:

"Hell, ...and then you realize that life is a joke, that you have no friends around. You realize that you have been alone all along and you start overanalyzing your feelings. You are feeling things so strongly and that makes you wish you never existed. You get paranoid, you feel that your end has come, and you desperately need someone to save you, but nobody is there... no friends, no family, no one.

Your mind takes a scary ride and plays wicked games on you. You think you are blank, and you start questioning your whole existence. You get lost in a deep abyss and black pictures fill your head. You think to yourself... 'Where are my friends? I want to see my family! Tell them all I love them!'

You think that you are about to die and the only way to calm yourself down is to accept that you are going to stop existing, that your life is about to end. You sharply close your eyes and scream goodbye to everything and everyone. You have regrets for all the things you have never done; you regret you never faced your fears. The day after, life changes color."

I believe that I went through a near-death experience. I don't wish anyone to experience such a thing, but as much as it hurt, it has changed me inside out and I wouldn't take it back.

The next day, I made a promise and I made a choice. I promised to God, to myself, to the world, that I will not take another day for granted.

I promised that I would appreciate my life and feel grateful for being alive every day. I promised that I would research, learn about and apply every single technique, exercise, and routine that exists, and can lead to a joyful life, a life of meaning, a life worth remembering. I promised I would respect myself, my body, my soul and my mind.

I asked God to show me the way to make this into reality and I dedicated myself to my personal development. I read every book I found on the topic, read every article and practiced every emotion-regulation technique I discovered. I chose to remove negativity from my life and to include as much positivity as I could.

I slowly turned my life around. I turned a life of negativity into a life of joy and bliss.

By making the above changes, I learned that our life experience is shaped by our choices. Our life experience is shaped by what we choose to cultivate inside.

I learned how to beat anxiety, fear, and sadness, and how to create peace, happiness, and love. Most importantly, the change I made inside allowed me to make reality all of my dreams.

Finally, the last promise I made was to help as many people as possible put an end to their misery, to teach them how to regulate their emotions, to help them accept themselves, see their own beauty and create a life worth living.

These are 15 steps that can help you turn your life around:

1. Learn how to feed yourself in the best possible way and learn about the importance of hydration. What you eat and drink have a strong impact on your emotions.
2. Move your body! The more you do, the more you will want to do it. Exercise in the right way for you. Find the type of exercise that fits you, relaxes you and makes you happy.
3. Add creativity in your life, e.g., paint, dance, sing, play music, write.
4. Reconnect with nature, connect with animals.
5. Work on your thoughts, switch your "worst case scenario" thinking to a "best case scenario" thinking.
6. Choose where you focus your attention. Choose what you read, hear and watch. Choose to experience positivity, cut down negativity.
7. Get rid of your faulty beliefs. In many cases, you are the one limiting yourself.
8. Stop complaining, stop criticizing! Talk about dreams, talk about ideas, talk about positive change.
9. Be grateful for all the things you are taking for granted. Say thank you, express your appreciation every day!

10. Do small acts of kindness every day, it can have a huge impact on your mood.

11. Learn and practice relaxation, meditation and visualization. Use positive affirmations, talk to yourself in a nice way.

12. Listen to your intuition, don't ignore it! All the answers are inside of you.

13. Take time to write down your goals for every area of your life (the big goals).

14. Before you sleep, write down the things you want to achieve the next day (the small goals). Break down the big goals and take action.

15. Celebrate your successes, even the smallest ones! Celebrate yourself!

About Dr. Anna Pavlina

Dr. Anna Pavlina Charalambous is the Founder of "Springs of Creation", which provides online as well as face-to-face educational and personal development services. The main aim of these services is to bring peace back to people through the application of different emotion regulation techniques, through creativity exercises and by raising awareness.

Pavlina's vision is to remind as many people as possible that they are the creators of their own life. She is a Certified Professional Life Coach and works with people that want to create balance and peace in their lives through the above-mentioned techniques and subsequently design their dream lives. She also works with creatives (musicians, actors, artists, dancers, and writers) that want to have emotional stability in their lives, become as successful as possible by first finding their balance, and then by making their vision into reality. She firmly believes that in order for someone to be the designer of their life, they first need to create peace inside. She is a highly empathetic individual, a true motivator, and a firm believer in the dreams of every human being. Working with her will give you a great supporter for the life you are capable of living.

Anna Pavlina Charalambous holds a PhD, an MSc and a BSc in Psychology, and has completed her eight-year-long studies in the United Kingdom. Since 2014, she has been working as a Lecturer at the University of Nicosia, Cyprus and has been teaching various courses including: Cognitive Psychology, Cognition and Emotion and Experimental Psychology. Since 2016, she has also started working as the Cyprus Research Coordinator for an H2020 European Project aiming to improve the mental wellbeing of elderly Europeans, in which the European University Cyprus and the University of Cyprus Centre for Applied Neuroscience, are partners. Her research interests include anxiety and anxiety disorders, mental well-being, personality, cognition and emotion relations and cognitive assessment.

In 2013, she started conducting and teaching numerous workshops and trainings for students, parents and teachers in many schools all around Cyprus as a trainer for different European Humanitarian Projects. In 2016, she created and started providing interactive workshops for the wider public on topics such as:

- ○ "How to deal with Anxiety"
- ○ "How to overcome your Fears"
- ○ "The Road to Happiness"
- ○ "What is Love?"
- ○ "How to apply Emotion Regulation Techniques"

The conduction of these trainings were driven by her desire to talk to the public about the different ways and techniques that can prevent the emergence of serious psychological problems.

You can connect with Dr. Anna Pavlina Charalambous at:
- • www.springsofcreation.com

CHAPTER 7

TUNE INTO YOUR DESTINY

BY AANCHAL VASHISTHA

What you think, you become. What you feel, you attract.
What you imagine, you create.
~ Buddha

If you are going to be successful in achieving your dreams, you have to stop wasting your time and energy on questions like 'What is my purpose?' or 'Why was I born?' There is only one answer to this question. Here it is:

Your purpose in life is to serve and to carry humanity forward by adding value to people's lives. Read that again. Tuning into this belief is the determining factor in the quality of life you will continue to live, and all the achievements you are yet to accomplish.

STOP WASTING TIME QUESTIONING WHAT YOUR PURPOSE IS!

The real questions you should be asking are: What do you want to serve? Whom do you want to serve? How do you want to serve? The rest will eventually come together once you truly tune into your destiny, with integrity and discipline.

We are born to be of service; whether it is to serve as an entrepreneur to fill a want or need; or whether it is to serve as an employee and add value to your employer's vision. In either case, you are helping people accomplish their goals and live a better life. No matter what industry or role you choose: actor, musician, painter, construction worker, coordinator, cleaner, technology, doctor, or lawyer, you are making a difference in someone's life. That is your purpose… for now. Also, this is your purpose until you find what you have been doing has now satisfied you and it is time to move on, or maybe it does not bring you joy anymore. Perhaps it is a sign to take a step back and realign with a new purpose.

I am a 27-year-old self-made humble millionaire. To some, that may not be a lot. To some that is remarkable because I chose to make the right choices to get to be in this position today. This journey has constant ups and downs, but the downs are what I call, 'growth points.'

While the passing of my twin brother Tushar three years ago to suicide has been a hard pill to swallow, I believe this tragedy was meant to happen in order to make me the person I am yet to become.

Fifteen years ago, my older brother, Prashant, had passed away to cerebral malaria in Nigeria. It broke my family apart for years. It took a decade to see my parents smile and engage in activities, go out for movies and hang out with friends again. However, time healed the wounds. Today when they talk about him, it is in an empowered tone rather than a victim language.

We don't have to spend ten years to heal. We can make a choice today to invest in becoming more aware of the state of our health – emotionally, physically, mentally, and spiritually – and take action to improve where we currently are.

FOCUS ON WHAT YOU DO WANT

I believe we are capable of achieving anything we set our minds to. We are not meant to stick to one job for the rest of our lives. There may be comfort in that, but there is no growth, no new environments or relationships, nothing that pushes you to explore your full potential. Even C-level executives and life-long entrepreneurs who have retired early have become artists, life coaches, healers, business coaches, or motivational speakers. They are constantly learning and moving on to the next thing to serve and uncover their potential. These people are super high-achievers.

My mentor, Jack Canfield, along with Mark Victor Hansen and Les Hewitt, published a book, *The Power of Focus*, for which they interviewed 1000 successful entrepreneurs to determine what separates them from normal everyday people. The three determining factors that they found were: (1) they had unusual clarity, (2) they have developed powerful, successful habits (disciples of success), and lastly, (3) they took 100% responsibility for their results and are action-oriented.

START TODAY

Start today by answering the following questions once a quarter or every month to check-in and realign:

1. What do you want to do to achieve?

_____

2. Where do you want to be?

_____

3. Within how much time?

_____

4. What emotions do you want to feel when you achieve your goal?

_____

5. Whom do you want around you or what kind of people do you want to be surrounded by?

_____

The more specific you are, the better it is. It trains your subconscious to make your thoughts a reality. The brain is such a powerful tool. However, many people do not utilize its full potential. People are afraid of change; often lazy, hesitant, and afraid of the unknown. That is where opportunities lie for progress. If you want to be a public speaker, chances are you would have to stand alone in front of the crowd in order to impact people and have them applaud you. So get used to working alone or traveling alone. Everything comes with a price and a payoff.

This is the process I follow to tune into my destiny. I call it P.R.R.O.P.

1. Practice Consistent Learning

Often what you want is tinted with limited beliefs or ideas that you are carrying, limiting beliefs you grew up with, including any behavioral traits that are generationally transmitted to you. Whether it is from birth, your upbringing, overbearing parents, or the environment you grew up in, it is a deep-seated conditioned belief. For example, thoughts like: I cannot, I must not, I do not, I have to, I am, I am not, people are, or he is not.

Henry Ford, an American industrialist, business magnate and founder of the Ford Motor Company, said, "Whether you think you can or think you can't, either way you are right." Your thoughts become your reality. Being open to new information and acknowledging brainwashed thoughts and correcting them, helps with clarifying what you want. When you improve your actions by seeking growth, it also empowers people in your network to do the same and helps the next generation not to witness similar behavioral patterns in you that you did not like growing up.

I either read or hear motivational self-help and mental health awareness books every morning to expand my knowledge. It keeps me motivated, excited to uncover more strategies, and sometimes to withdraw from projects that would not help me achieve my goals effectively. Constantly learning helps with determining what you want to do and provides clarity.

2. Reflect

After you are aware of your next destination, it is time to gain clarity and visualize your way to success. Visualization helps to stay in control, increases motivation, and tricks the brain to believe it is reality. Over time, possibilities present themselves, people will want to connect with you, and opportunities that could you take you to the next level show up.

At the age of 15, I became a silver medalist in Interstate Table Tennis in two categories – Girls Doubles and Girls Singles in 2007. The culture and environment I grew up in was different. There was a bigger disparity between girls versus boys and limited beliefs like boys can be rough and loud, whereas nice girls smile more, uplift people and do not get angry. Nice girls take care of their family. There were not a lot of girls in my school who participated in sports. They were not encouraged to either.

I was blessed with two brothers growing up. My late older brother Prashant would encourage me to play sports. In my school growing up, I participated in everything and anything that my school offered, whether I had any knowledge of it or not. Whether it was track and field, arts and crafts, dancing, singing or mime competitions, I would just try. Before every single event started, I used to feel shy, uncomfortable, and anxious. I didn't want people to look at me, but I felt the fear and tried it anyway. I lost a few times but also won quite a bit. When I lost, I took it as a sign of growth, reflected on how I could improve, asked questions, practiced, visualized myself winning, the crowd clapping for me, and I came back even stronger. When I would win, I would make time to celebrate every win, but also reflect on the accomplishment, take notes on what others did that I found valuable, and still kept improving.

Reflection helps with aligning and realigning your vision so you can tune into your destiny.

3. Reach Out Together

Nothing can stop us but us. No blessing is a blessing if you can't handle it. Think about it. If you cannot figure out how to get up when you are down, you will not know how to handle yourself when you are successful. A lot of celebrities, influencers, and politicians who have achieved great levels of success, are still not happy. Do what it takes to help you move forward mentally. If you do not feel good, go to therapy like you go to the gym. Your mental health is as important as your physical health. If you are finding it difficult to schedule your first appointment, reach out to someone that you trust and can help you book the first meeting.

A lot of people will not understand. Some people will leave when you are going through a rough time mentally, emotionally, financially, or physically. Those people are not your support system. If you broke your hand, you would not ask your partner to fix it for you. You would go to the doctor to get it reset. When you are not feeling well mentally for a prolonged time, your immediate circle may not even know how to help you. Find your support, including professional support. You are the driver of your life, whether it was your fault or not; choose a response that will bring you joy. Reach out for professional help, pick up a self-help book, and take time to meditate, exercise, and force yourself to leave your house every day.

4. Own Your Choices With Confidence

I founded Reach Out Together, a Canadian Mental Health Awareness not-for-profit organization in 2017 in Canada, six months after my twin brother had passed away to suicide. If I had not stood up for my well being and myself, I would not be in a position to run it and inspire the world through my talks.

I left a job in technology where I was very happy, growing and financially well. But my thirst to keep making more money no longer seemed to be my purpose anymore. I chose to get certified as a Mental Health First Aider with the Mental Health Commission Of Canada, took courses in social entrepreneurship at the Centre for Social Innovation, invested in becoming Canfield Certified in the Success Principles with my mentor, Jack Canfield, to help people tune into their destiny. There was no laid out path. I am creating that path everyday with intention.

5. Practice Mindfulness

Have you noticed those thoughts that are always running at the back of your mind? They are subconscious thoughts that can intentionally be made conscious through training. Two tools I practice every day to be aware of my thoughts are meditation and talking to myself positively in front of a mirror. In the beginning, it may seem awkward and pointless. But if you can stay consistent and practice meditating a minimum of once a day in the morning and end the night with positive self-talk in front of a mirror, for a minimum of 40 days, you will notice a huge difference in your automatic self-talk. You will become more aware of those negative thoughts or behaviors about yourself that are deep conditioned.

TUNE INTO YOUR DESTINY

Robert Collier, the American author of the Best-Selling book, *The Secret Of The Ages*, said, "Our subconscious minds have no sense of humor, play no jokes and cannot tell the difference between reality and an imagined thought or image. What we continually think about eventually will manifest in our lives."

Live life with passion and excitement; engage in activities with a full heart. If you do something, do it well or do not do it at all. Life is too short to work or live in misery. We are here to carry humanity forward; let's do the best we can today, visualize a better tomorrow and behave as if your attitude will determine your level of success. Redefine where do you want to go. It is never too late or early to start.

About Aanchal

Aanchal Vashistha is an award-winning international speaker, author, Certified Canfield Trainer in the Success Principles™, Certified Mental Health First Aider and social entrepreneur. She moves audiences around the world as she advocates for life after trauma, resilience, success, youth and workplace wellness.

Her career started in technology working at Citibank and moved to a digital advertising network. She also worked as a freelance consultant helping organizations with their branding and communications strategy. Six months after the passing of her twin brother to suicide; Aanchal founded Reach Out Together, a Canadian not-for-profit organization to encourage people to maintain good mental health through educational programs.

Aanchal is also the co-author of *101 Unconventional Strategies* and leads mindset transformational training for workplaces, schools, and other community groups. Aanchal is passionate about uncovering her full potential while training people in her community to do the same. She truly believes in the power of community reaching out together to heal, to move forward and to create a life that brings people joy, health, and wealth.

She has appeared frequently in the media and as a guest speaker at several events including EmpowerCon at the Los Angeles Convention Center, The Global Love Ambassador Summit at Metro Hall Toronto, as well as at other memorable events in Nigeria, Canada, United States and India.

Aanchal received an EXPY® Award at the Annual ThoughtLeader Summit for her accomplishments as an entrepreneur, expert and professional, in Hollywood, California on September 25, 2019. She also received the Community Development Award on October 6, 2019 at the African Scholar's Award Ceremony at the University of Toronto.

You can connect with Aanchal directly at:
- Email: aanchvash@gmail.com or aanchal@reachouttogether.com
- Social Media: @AanchalVash or @ROTambassador

CHAPTER 8

THREE ESSENTIAL PASSWORDS TO GO FROM IMPOSSIBLE TO UNSTOPPABLE

BY JAMIE DeNOVO

Alice: "I simply must get through!"
Doorknob: "Sorry, you're much too big. Simply impassable."
Alice: "You mean IMPOSSIBLE?"
Doorknob: "No, impassable. Nothing's Impossible."
~ Alice in Wonderland by Lewis Carroll

It was a dark and stormy night. As the clock struck midnight, the exhausted author sat alone in her office, hunched over a humming computer, eyes blurred, oblivious to all but the screen. The kids had been packed off to their grandparents. Her husband was locked in the basement. She had been working madly for weeks to condense 4,000 complex brain science research white papers into one 2,000-word recipe that could save the planet. There were only six hours left in the deadline for presentation to the United Nations. One more paragraph and the thing was done. The sun could come out tomorrow, the banished family could return, the world would be a better place.

Then, the computer crashed.

Has that ever happened to you? Maybe not all of it, but the part where you are working on an important project and suddenly your computer starts misbehaving? If there are too many files open, or incompatible software, the device can't process it all properly, and begins to crash. You get the little 'Circle of Dread' that keeps going round and round. The more you try to stop it, the worse things get. Finally, up pops "This program is not responding." Now the whole system is stuck. It needs a restart. And often you need a refresh to integrate new information with what you already have and see what it looks like. At times like this, it doesn't matter what we had planned or had to accomplish for whom. Until we get our system back in order, we can't get past 'GO'. That process takes time, patience and the ability to move calmly and productively through frustration.

It doesn't matter if you're the most positive person in the world, ready to save the day, there isn't anyone on the planet who doesn't get stuck and need a restart every once in a while. The ability to reset and thrive in the face of chaos and uncertainty is an essential part of our everyday lives. Not just so we can act effectively under challenge or when things go sideways, but in order to stay sane and maintain healthy priorities. Sometimes it's one big thing. Sometimes it's a hundred little things that pile up until you feel you can't cope a moment longer. Despite our best efforts, we come up against a wall that won't move. Or a goal that keeps moving out of reach. We give it all we've got, but eventually begin to view the situation as hopeless, impossible. Like Alice in the opening quote, we confuse 'impassible' with 'impossible.' But when we know how to direct our brain, options come into focus.

What are some of the things that make people feel they are in an impossible situation? We might feel physically trapped in a home, neighborhood, relationship, workplace, or community that we desperately want to leave. We can become emotionally locked in by tradition, habit, addiction or expectations (our own or someone else's). Physical or mental conditions, spiritual despondency or disillusionment, lack of finances, the past, even a culture or lifestyle, can cause us to feel imprisoned and helpless to break free.

> *Most of the important things in the world have been*
> *accomplished by people who have kept on trying*
> *when there seemed to be no hope at all.*
> ~ Dale Carnegie

How can we move forward, not just once but again and again, in the face of overwhelming frustration, fear, discouragement, failure and setbacks - even victimization? When you understand some very basic concepts about how the brain works, how you can reset your brain and change your reality at any moment, that's when you can "superpower" your ability to climb out of any mental black hole.

What makes my book and the I.M.Possible Muscle program different from all the others? Glad you asked. I wrote the book because I couldn't find the information anywhere else. I've read all the books, taken the courses, lived the life, and walked the talk. Then suddenly, my world crashed. I was catapulted into a place where none of the rules for success and fair play applied. It was like being pushed into a deep abyss surrounded by fluid walls that give way at a touch. There were no solid handholds anywhere to climb out. I realized then what all those experts were missing. Life isn't as simple as grand gestures, rules and platitudes. You can do all the right things in all the right ways and still have it go wrong because life doesn't play fair. At that point, inspirational stories just made me feel worse. So now what? All the books teach that you have to believe to achieve. What if I don't believe anymore? What if I believe but it's not working? Where was the talk for ground subzero? Therapists couldn't give it to me, and friends, family – they just didn't know how to help. There was no talk to walk. No one had it. I literally had to create the missing handholds or die. So, I started walking, injured and ill-equipped. It was my seemingly impossible trek into uncharted territory that produced the missing talk. I found answers experts had missed in places no one had thought of looking. And while I might not have saved the world, I found a way to climb out of the grave and make a joyful difference in my own world and that of countless others. I make it possible for anyone, anywhere, to short-circuit their circle of dread, reset, and achieve worthy goals that once seemed impossible…And that's a pretty good start.

"I.M.Possible and the I.M.Possible processes gave me, and will give anyone who is stuck for the first time or the hundredth time or the thousandth, a way to become unstoppable."
~ Bradley Scheele
(client, author, owner of a large medical practice)

DOING THE IMPOSSIBLE: IT'S LIKE BUILDING MUSCLE

Athletes become stronger the more they work out and train towards their goal. They can condition themselves and their muscles to respond reflexively through practice and technique. The brain works the same way. I.M.Possible and I.M.Possible Muscle concepts take you to the very heart of how the brain works. The techniques train you how to move your feet and your brain when they're stuck. When we get stuck and can't seem to move forward, it's a signal to get the body to reset and move and the brain to do the same. To do that, there's something that needs to happen to us physically and mentally. It's something we can make happen, but it's not something that automatically or naturally happens. The I.M.Possible processes focus on the moment you are stuck – on how get your feet and your brain moving in the right direction, so you can pull out of the mental mire.

Anyone who has ever created a big-picture success against the odds has unconsciously built and trained some aspect of their I.M.Possible muscle. They've hit places where they've gone,

"How do I reset my thinking to get past the roadblock in front of me right now?" And consciously or not, they've used the 'Fiber by Fiber' and 'One Sock Processes', which I've outlined in my book, *I.M.Possible Muscle for The Mind*. Like building physical muscle stamina and flexibility, it's all dynamics that work together to get you and your brain on the same team. In moment-by-moment steps, not complex or huge leaps, I coach you through ways to get your brain unstuck in any situation. Practice with these techniques will power your ability to change your reality in the moment, and achieve positive outcomes under even the most challenging circumstances – even when the obstacles seem impassible, and success seems impossible.

My book isn't a book – it's a guide to building your brain. It will serve you forever. What you learn, you will own. And we all need to own this knowledge. Because life is messy. It's always something: new or old trials, or both. When you master the art of resetting your brain over and over again, rejection, failure, and setbacks become a normal part of the process. They won't stop you from moving forward.

Here are three techniques you can use right now to start building an unstoppable brain.

1. THE MINDSHIFT: REDEFINE IMPOSSIBLE, REINVENT POSSIBLE.

What is I.M.Possible? I.M.Possible is *the process of making possible* what appears now as impossible. Before now, there was no word to define the process of transition whereby a condition that was defined as *impossible* is proven to be, or is made, *possible*. The brain cannot think something is possible and impossible simultaneously. But it can think *I.M.Possible*, meaning *I Make Possible*. The concept *makes way* for neural networks to override limiting beliefs about what is possible and impossible. You can now consider solutions and create positive outcomes that you had formerly believed to be impossible.

"Why, the best way to explain it is to do it!"
~ The Dodo in *Through the Looking Glass* by Lewis Carrol

Words, even those you say to yourself, carry the potential to act on brain networks in such a powerful way, that they can change the direction of your day—and even your life! Do you find this hard to believe??? Take the challenge as outlined below and experience for yourself, right now, the power of words.

A. Take a deep breath and close your eyes. Filter out everything else and focus completely on what is going on inside of you.

B. Think the word **"IMPOSSIBLE."** It's a powerful word. Listen to your internal response. Now say the word out loud IMPOSSIBLE. Say it again, …and again.

C. Now, say the following out loud, "This is going to be an IMPOSSIBLE day. Today, in everything I do I will think "IMPOSSIBLE."

How do you feel? Write down your thoughts and feelings—physical, mental, emotional— when you say those words.

Now, repeat the same procedure, but this time change the word "IMPOSSIBLE" to "I.M.POSSIBLE."

Take a deep breath, close your eyes and focus internally.

Think the word **"I.M.POSSIBLE."** Pronounce out loud, **"I-M-POSSIBLE"** meaning **"I-Make-Possible."** Say it three more times.

Say aloud, clearly, "This is a going to be an **I.M.Possible** day. Today in everything I do I will think **I.M.Possible.**"

Now how do you feel? List the physical, mental and emotional sensations that come with your words.

I first gave the above test to 20 people from different walks of life and have since tested hundreds more. If you took the test seriously, your responses to the above will be very similar to theirs. Impossible is a mental wall word. The brain connects it with 'No Go' thoughts and emotions. I.M.Possible ignites action-oriented brain networks. I'll make possible! Your brain responds accordingly, producing thoughts and emotions that support your ability to make a positive outcome whatever challenges the day brings!

2. PASSAGE THROUGH: WHEN YOU CAN'T THINK POSITIVE

Your world has fallen apart. You are in emotional crisis. What do you hear? "You've just got to quit thinking negative. It's bad energy. Think positive." How helpful is that? Ironically, this well-meaning advice often has the opposite effect. Out come the mental boxing gloves! Why is that?

For our brain, shifting emotional gears from stalled to high is hugely challenging, especially when underlying issues are deep and unresolved. Our thoughts and emotions have no way to make the transition to the concept "positive." The brain can't associate happy with distressed. Unsurprisingly, our internal response is defensive. The teeth grind. We think, "Really? You have no idea. Don't minimize my pain!" Do you see how 'as it flows it grows'? As emotions bring thoughts, thoughts amplify emotions. They feed off each other and grow. So, what would act as a handhold we could reach during times like this? How could we begin to climb upward? Instead of 'think positive', let's try the friendly advice again, using a "think productive" approach.

"I don't blame you for feeling the way you do. It's a challenging situation, but negative thoughts just hurt you more. I want to help you move forward. So, what is the most productive thing you can think of to do right now?" The idea of productive thinking doesn't underplay our pain or diminish our challenge. It doesn't suggest our problem is merely one of mood. Whatever the cause of our suffering, we do generally recognize that we want to somehow stop things from getting worse, which would be counterproductive.

Productive thinking gives us something to do. It activates motivational as well as reward-producing brain circuits. Being productive makes us feel better, pulls us out of a stall. We now have a means to create an emotional transition to a more positive place. Our brain begins to change enough to reset our focus and direction. Productive actions enable us to advance, in tiny but progressive steps, from chaos to coherence to achievement.

3. GETTING UNSTUCK: GET OFF YOUR 'BUT'

When life gets frustrating, do you ever find yourself saying, "I'm trying to achieve this outcome, but..." or, "I have to finish this, but..." or, "I really shouldn't do this, but..."? Remember, words powerfully impact our brain. *While the word "impossible" creates a mental wall, "but" forms one of the bricks*. Of course, there is a time for wall words, *but* when we need to get past the wall, they are best used with caution. The word *"but"* causes the firing of neurotransmitters in regions that restrict or inhibit action associated with its object. These network to produce emotions supporting the 'dead end' message. When passage through is critical, the mental 'Circle of Dread' starts spinning. What will help to keep your brain solution oriented?

Go back to the beginning of the section and this time, replace the word *"but"* with the word *"so."* What happens? Do you feel the difference in your mind? *So* is a natural bridge word, not a brick wall. It focuses us *toward* the goal. You signal your brain network to search out ways to get there. *So* is a *think productive* support word. What is the result? Your mind becomes much more receptive to conditions or information that support a positive outcome.

94

The next time you find yourself saying, "I would, *but...*" remember: To keep sitting on a *but* makes it grow. To make your but disappear, move off it and do something else. Make it *so.*

So, what happened to our harried hero of the dark and stormy night and the villainous computer?

The beleaguered author screamed, "Impossible! This is not happening! But I..." All that brain research, however, wasn't wasted on our hero... One thing she *could* stop from crashing was her brain. Shifting into I.M.Possible Muscle gear, she took a deep breath (sending oxygen to the brain) and focused on solutions. *Think productive. So...* yes! That was it! On her phone, she googled how to retrieve unsaved documents after a crash, successfully recouping all but the last three paragraphs! The fractured family was happily reunited.

The United Nations, however, is another story...

No, I don't pretend to have answers to everything (especially technology). That *is* an impossible thing to do. What I can promise is this: As you build your I.M.Possible Muscle, you will absolutely increase your power and ability to get unstuck, identify solutions and make passage through to the best possible outcomes in whatever situation you face. Amazing, wonder-filled outcomes that would otherwise remain in the realm of the impossible.

Start by doing what's necessary; then do what's possible;
and suddenly you are doing the Impossible.
~ St. Francis of Assisi

About Jamie

Jamie DeNovo is a passionate and multi-talented entrepreneur, author, brain science researcher, public speaker and coach. Jamie's mission is to help people facing personal or professional crisis to win the greatest battle they will ever face – the war within. Jamie understands that knowing what to do means nothing if you just can't do it. Getting stuck is the biggest obstacle any of us have in creating success and long-term solutions. *We miss out on achieving the life we could have had.* Jamie's I.M.Possible Muscle program and pioneering techniques teach clients how to remap brain pathways and move forward productively through overload, confusion, trauma, crisis or any other situation presenting mental and emotional roadblocks.

As an entrepreneur and corporate executive for 25 years, Jamie's expertise in success against long odds is grounded in first-hand experience. In the late 1990's, Jamie and her husband transformed their home-based electronics repair business into a niche security company with an elite reputation for design and manufacture of proprietary, leading-edge video capture solutions. Jamie's visionary direction and support foundation, paired with gold standard technology and service, attracted prestigious clients from the world's hardest-to-penetrate market sectors – Homeland Security and Law Enforcement covert operations. As Director of Special Projects, for 10 years Jamie travelled between Calgary, Canada and Washington, D.C., where she built and maintained relationships with clients ranging from field agents to White House executives.

When faced with life-threating PTSD, Jamie DeNovo took her career in a new direction. Enlisting the support of one of the world's most revered neuroscientists, Dr. Bryan Kolb, Jamie's search for answers eventually established her place as a pioneer in maximizing human potential. Over a period of four years, while living each step, Jamie developed the book, *I.M.Possible Muscle for the Mind*, a game-changing universal micro-blueprint for positive change and achievement beyond belief. Jamie is the originator of revolutionary concepts such as: *I.M.Possible, I.M.Possible Muscle, The One Sock Process* and *Optimal Victory.*

You can contact Jamie at:
- jamie@jamiedenovo.com
- https://ca.linkedin.com/pub/jamie-denovo/64/15b/579

CHAPTER 9

TIME MANAGEMENT STRATEGIES
TAKE CONTROL OF YOUR MANIC SCHEDULE

BY ALLIE JORGENSEN

TIME MANAGEMENT SYSTEM FOR MUSICIANS

The lure of the music industry conjures up visual images of huge stages with massive crowds and living the high life of the Rock and Roll Music lifestyle. However, the reality is so much different than we all imagine. The 60 minutes that you are on stage, feeling that incredible connection with your music and your audience constitutes only a small part of what the music business really consists of. The true story for many is quite different from the fairytale we all envision.

My childhood started out in a relatively modest living environment and I left home at a young age to escape an alcoholic mother. After I left my toxic world, I ended up in a one-room shack in Hollywood, CA eating Ramen noodles with no more than my wits and my background in music to survive. I was extremely fortunate that certain people appeared in my environment to give me advice and help get me on track, and assist with the business side of things just when I needed them. I was able to go from eating Ramen noodles in a shack in Hollywood, CA, to actually winning a Music award and having a song selected as a theme song for a film. However, with a background in the music industry, both as a performance Artist and working behind the scenes later in my life, with a successful music magazine, I can tell you first-hand that there are very real issues with anxiety created by feelings of overwhelm and loss of time management. It became apparent in my own life that I would need to begin to apply new strategies or lose myself in a state of becoming overwhelmed.

Time is our most valuable resource, and mastering time management is the difference between being busy and being productive. It doesn't matter who you are – there are still only 24 hours in a day. That is why it is essential to have effective time management strategies. We are pulled in so many directions and we have so many demands placed on our personal and professional lives, but what if there was a way to bring a higher level of efficiency to our lives that included more free time? What if you were able to focus on achieving your goals instead of checking an endless to-do list? This would change the quality of your life and open up much more free time for yourself.

In the case of touring musicians, those who employ an effective time management system and master time management are living richer fuller lives in contrast to those who are struggling with overwhelming anxiety. As schedules get busier and more hectic, there is less free time and it's harder to get enough done in the amount of time that you do have. There are constant distractions and you are forever sidetracked, making it near impossible to tackle your endless to-do's. In an industry with never-ending demands on your time, it is more important than ever to establish a strategy of effective time management, including setting boundaries for "Me" time.

One of the key components for me, was to take a step back and SLOW DOWN. The pace becomes so frantic and hectic that you can lose sight of what's important and what can wait until later. This is where effective time management comes into play. Many of the techniques that I utilized back then in my life, I would later use to create a complete strategic system for time management, which, in reality, was created out of my own need for peace of mind. After I transitioned out of the performance side of the music industry, and founded an in-depth online music magazine, I noticed when talking to many musicians during interviews for the magazine, that they were struggling with the same issues I had once struggled with.

I became extremely passionate about this endless problem when I lost a dear friend to suicide, because she was caught up in the stress and overwhelming demands of the industry. I then began to study and research different aspects of how the brain works, and I became fascinated by Neuroscience research and the study of Neuro-technology – which opens the gateway to understanding the brain and various aspects of consciousness and thought, as well as technologies that are designed to improve brain function.

As I began to study Neuroscience, my studies led me to Neuro-Linguistic Programing and the decision to become a Certified NLP Practitioner and a Certified Transformational Life Coach. But there was more to the puzzle than just managing your time, there was something missing. I began to realize that to have an effective strategy for time management, I needed to shift my focus and begin to transform my entire mindset by turning off the noise, eliminating busy work, and gaining crystal-clear clarity.

So, based on what I learned, here are seven (7) steps to achieving an effective and successful time management strategy, and a powerful and proven formula for ultimate Time Management. I have applied this process to my own life as well as the life of my clients. The key components of the strategy are as follows:

1. WRITE IT DOWN – PROCESS OF CHUNKING

KEEP A ONE-WEEK DIARY – KEEP TRACK OF WHERE YOU SPEND YOUR TIME – BOTH BUSINESS AND PERSONAL.

To begin the chunking process, you must get the ideas out of your head and onto paper. Write down everything you have to do this week. Consider this a complete brain dump for your thoughts.

- Separate into two columns – Business and Personal.

  o Business Column: Finances, Work, Career, Mission and Marketing – Creativity can go into both columns depending on the application.

  o Personal Column: Relationships, Life Mastery, Health and Fitness, Emotions and Spirituality.

- Find those items on your list that take up most of your time and prioritize them based on your goals and purpose.

- Look for "Time Suckers": These are some of the things you are spending too much time on, and ask yourself – do they provide as much value as I would like?
  (Items like scrolling social media and Netflix binging – limit these items to your stress-free time.)

2. YOUR FOCUS

FOCUS IS THE ULTIMATE POWER THAT CAN CHANGE THE WAY WE THINK, THE WAY WE FEEL AND WHAT WE DO IN ANY MOMENT. WHEN WE CHANGE OUR FOCUS, WE CHANGE OUR LIFE.

- After you chunk pieces together, shift your mindset to focus on a brilliant future. Too often we forget what our result

102

or outcome is, and we start thinking about what we don't have, instead of thinking about how to make things happen to create what we do want to have.

• Get crystal clear about what it is that you want. Then you can design all of your activity around making progress toward achieving it. The clearer you are about what it is you want, the easier it is to achieve it.

• Whatever the outcome may be, your brain can figure out how to get there and your behavior will adjust accordingly.

• There are so many things competing for your attention in life, so you have to make a conscious effort to decide in advance which things you're going to focus on, or you'll live in reaction to demands of the moment.

3. <u>MINDSET AND MINDFULNESS</u>

THESE TWO STEPS TOGETHER HELP TO RE-WIRE YOUR BRAIN TO GET YOUR POWER BACK.

• MINDFULNESS is a mental state achieved by focusing one's awareness on the present moment, calmly focusing and acknowledging one's feelings, thoughts, and bodily sensations, including breathing techniques. Be conscious of how you are feeling and ACKNOWLEDGE how you are feeling – good or bad. Take the time to breathe and slow down your heart rate.

• MINDSET is where you *Control Your Self Talk* and *Really Believe* in yourself. The mind is the key to your sustained success. Even a great strategy won't succeed without the right mindset to implement it. When you change your mindset, you are then able to transform your life.

• According to Neuroscience researchers, positive thinking can influence our lives. The impact positive thoughts can have on your future has been proven in the past two decades. However, you have to remove negative thinking from your life and actively practice positive thinking on a daily basis, as positive thinking is not something that "Just Happens".

• You need to find ways to cultivate and nurture optimism in your life; stay away from the "Dark Hole" of social media and press reviews.

4. <u>PURPOSE – WHAT IS YOUR WHY?</u>

DO YOU KNOW THE REASON WHY YOU WANT TO CREATE THIS OUTCOME?

• Get absolutely clear on why you are doing your music or art and ask yourself: Do you still love what you do?

• Who is your message for? Is it to help others in need?

• What groups do you reach and how can you help them even more?

• How can you become an even better Leader?

• When you establish your purpose, it is easier to see the result you desire. You will need to associate your purpose for wanting to achieve a certain result, and then you can focus on what you really want (i.e., your result or outcome).

• This is one of the most important parts of the process because without it you lose your emotional drive and you have more stress. This can cause you to give up when the challenges arise. But if you've got a strong-enough reason and a strong-enough purpose, you will find a way to pull it off. Whether or not you keep trying depends on your purpose – and when you feel inspired by a purpose, you'll come up with a more effective action plan to get there.

5. ACTION PLAN – Create Your "Chief Aim" GOAL

Best-Selling Author, Napoleon Hill, states that in order to attract what you want in life, you have to embed your goal deeply into your subconscious.

- Get clear on your "Chief Aim" GOAL. You need to write that chief aim down.

- Each morning and each night you should read your chief aim aloud and visualize it as if it has already happened.

- Really feel the amazing feelings you will feel once you have achieved your goal, embedding it firmly into your vision. Your subconscious will end up attracting opportunities for you to bring that Chief Aim GOAL to life.

- Powerful visualization techniques are the key.

6. ACCOUNTABILITY

- You will need an accountability partner or Coach who will help you set goals, identify what's holding you back and learn to move past fear.

- Your accountability partner or Coach should be someone with a background in the music industry who is well aware of the day-to-day challenges in the business. (Someone who will hold you accountable and not let you "Slide".)

- The mind is the key to your sustained success. Most people are held back by their own limiting beliefs and trapped in a cycle of negative self-talk.

- With an accountability partner or coach, you can change your mindset.

7. <u>ULTIMATE OUTCOME</u>

- When you're driven by your ultimate purpose, instead of the need to check items off a to-do list, you'll feel more productive and less stressed. When you feel less stressed, you find more reasons to act instead of making excuses.

- Most of us know what to do, but don't take the actions to follow through on our goals. We tell ourselves we're not brave enough. What holds everyone back is not their capabilities – it's the fear of failure. It's ok to be afraid, but it is not ok to let fear stop you. Set your goals, identify what's holding you back and learn to move past fear.

With these steps you can learn how to take incredible action and commit in times of uncertainty. Stepping out of your comfort zone is where the real growth happens.

You can create massive change in your life, if you have the courage to take the first step.
~ Allie Jorgensen

About Allie

Allie Jorgensen is the Founder and CEO of a premier online Company specializing in effective Time Management Strategies for Musicians called: **Time Management Solution Signature Program**, (www.TimeManagementSolution.com). This exclusive Signature Program gives Musicians more time in their schedule and alleviates stress and overwhelm so they can focus on what matters most to them and take back control of their schedules and lives. Allie helps Musicians master their Time Management so they can overcome the anxiety and overwhelm created by their hectic and manic schedules in the music industry. Her passion is to help Musicians get their time back, relieve their stress and have more time to spend with their families.

Allie is an Author, a Jack Canfield Certified Success and Life Coach, Certified NLP Practitioner, as well as a Speaker and Trainer.

Allie grew up on the streets of Hollywood, CA in the Music Industry, so she is only too familiar with the day-to-day challenges musicians face. After turning her life around from eating Ramen noodles in a shack in Hollywood, CA, she became an award-winning singer/songwriter, had her song selected as the theme song for a movie soundtrack, and became the Founder of a successful International Music Magazine.

Allie has spent many hours working with Top Musicians and Celebrities in the Music and Entertainment industries and is considered an expert when it comes to effective *Time Management Strategies* in the Music Industry.

Allie's book, *How To Survive The Music Industry*, is a step-by-step survival guide for anyone in the Music Business. She has worked with various organizations such as Rockers Against Cancer Society, Los Angeles Music Awards, Loudwire Music Awards, Century Media Records, Nuclear Blast Records, Napalm Records, Cleopatra Records and Universal Music Group. As an NLP Practitioner and Certified Life Coach and Trainer, Allie's research and training in Neuroscience has enabled her to create a powerful, proven and effective *Time Management* system that she uses in her own life as well as the lives of her clients.

In addition, to her passion for helping Musicians and giving back to that Industry, Allie is also passionate about helping teachers and students. Allie is certified from the Center for Teacher Effectiveness as a Trainer and Speaker in the area of Student Motivation and Student Engagement and delivers presentations to schools, districts and conferences. Allie combines her background in the Music Industry with her background in Education for an entertaining and thought-provoking presentation.

Allie has been featured on the cover of *Pulse Magazine* and also featured on the television talk show, *Actors Entertainment*, in Hollywood, CA.

You can connect with Allie Jorgensen at:
- www.TimeManagementSolution.com
- www.AllieJorgensen.com

CHAPTER 10

THE ROAD MAP TO SUCCESS

BY FIA JOHANNSON

DESIRE IS ONLY THE FIRST STEP

You probably bought this book because you want to be successful. Which I am glad you do! Almost everyone we know wants to be successful, but why do only a few achieve the great success we all envy? Now, I need to tell you right off the bat, there is nothing special about wanting to be successful.

Maybe it sounds harsh, and I don't mean for it to. But here is a truth that we need to come to grips with, and if we're honest with ourselves, it's something we already know deep down – *simply wanting to be successful is not enough!*

Everybody wants to be successful. Think about it. What child has ever laid in bed at night dreaming of someday when they would fail? Or what college freshman enrolls in their chosen major because they hope to someday feel stuck in their career? Who attends conferences designed to help them not live up to their dreams and aspirations? As humans, we are programmed to be positive and expect positive results. That is exactly why we start just about everything imaginable in our life. Even when the experience is a negative one, we start with the "hope" of achieving better results. Does anyone start anything expecting a negative result?

No, no one does, of course!

Everybody *wants* to be successful, but so many people end up living lives where success seems hard to attain. We feel like there's something more for us, something bigger, but we just don't know how to get to it. We have dreams in our hearts, but they feel too difficult, too unlikely, too far off.

Contrary to what most self-help gurus and marketing brands will tell you – desire is not enough to be successful, you have to have *strategies before patience and perseverance...*

Imagine you wanted to drive to visit the Grand Canyon (...and who wouldn't). You pack your bags, fill your car with gas, and get your favorite music or podcast ready for the drive. You get up early one morning, jump in the car, and just start driving in whatever direction felt right. And imagine if the whole time you were driving, you just kept telling yourself how much you *wanted* to get to the Grand Canyon. Imagine you put a picture of the Grand Canyon on the dashboard. You tell your closest friends and relatives that it has been your desire to go to the Grand Canyon all your life. Maybe you even began praying that you would get to the Grand Canyon? Perhaps you even paid some experts to tell you about the Grand Canyon and how it would be once you got there.

Would you get there?

Nope, not likely! Why? Because without the right strategies, you have no idea where you're going to end up, regardless of your desire. You have to start with a clear roadmap as to how you will get to the image you should have hacked in your mind, of the person, situation, or circumstances you need to create, to get where you want to go. This road map cannot necessarily be based on your current reality and what you "know" to be the only way to get to what you want.

In this chapter, I want to give you some strategies that can help you to actually achieve the success you desire. Whether you're a CEO, the founder of a start-up, a freelancer, or a small business owner, these are proven tactics that will lead you to the place you're hoping to go. And I can show you how to be successful because I've been there, and along the way I discovered that the so-called experts left out much of the details I experienced along the way. I have had to start over from scratch multiple times in my life, and each time I found myself at square one, I put these strategies into practice, and I have always found my way back to success.

The one driving desire was to find the doors to success despite being left alone in a dark room with no idea as to which way to start moving. To return to our earlier illustration: I've been to the Grand Canyon many times, and can show you the way instead of telling you about the greatness of the place and what you'd experience once you get there! I will leave that for you to experience it yourself.

I've walked this road many times and it has become my life's passion to help other people walk it, as well. I want to help you get to your Grand Canyon, I want to help you achieve your dreams, and this chapter is your roadmap to getting there.

MIND AND BODY INNER BALANCE

The first place to start is with the most important piece of the whole journey... **YOU!** That's right. You are the most important piece in your journey towards success. In our Grand Canyon analogy, you are the car. You can't get very far if the car breaks down!

"What happens in Vegas, stays in Vegas." We've all heard this famous slogan for Las Vegas, Nevada, the "City of Sin." In the mind of the ad agency that came up with it, this phrase was about *freedom*. Freedom to be who you want and do what you want, without it ever affecting your "real life" back home. The idea is simple and profound: you can separate your private life from your public life.

And the truth is that many of us buy into the "Vegas mindset" in our business. We think… "who I am at home has nothing to do with who I am at work." We believe our public life is completely separated from our private life. And it's understandable why we believe this; we need to believe it because we don't have time to pursue health at home! In the crazy world of the 21st century marketplace, most of the time we feel like we're just trying to keep up with everyone else. And so, we start putting off the things that are most important to us. "I'll spend more time with my kids as soon as this next deal is closed." "I'll start eating healthy as soon as we finish this project." "I'll exercise next quarter." In other words, in my private life I can sacrifice and it won't affect my business.

As enticing as this idea may be, of course, we all know that this is just not true. Very rarely does Vegas stay in Vegas, and very rarely does our compartmentalized life stay compartmentalized. Stress at home leads to less productivity. In their 2017 Global Benefits Attitudes Survey, Willis Towers Watson recorded that employees who are in the poorest health more than doubled their number of absences, were more than twice as likely to be disengaged from their jobs, and reported much higher stress levels than those in good health.[*] In other words, your personal health has an effect on your bottom line.

You can't make it to the Grand Canyon if your car breaks down.

---

[*] Willis Towers Watson, "2017 Global Benefits Attitudes Survey", p. 11. https://www.willistowerswatson.com/en-US/Insights/2017/11/2017-global-benefits-attitudes-survey-health-and-well-being

THE ROAD MAP TO SUCCESS

You have to pursue holistic health to succeed in the 21st century marketplace. If you want to lead an organization, you have to begin by leading yourself. The most important person in your life is you. You must take care of yourself if you want to make a difference!

Pursue mindfulness exercises, eat healthy, stay active, start a hobby, spend time with your family. If you want more practical tips on how to pursue personal, holistic health, grab a copy of my book, *Re-Coding Your Brain for a Better Life*. Don't buy into the lie that what happens at home stays at home. Get healthy!

STOP BLAMING

Have you ever been on a road trip with family or a friend? At some point, I can almost guarantee you, something went wrong. You either took a wrong turn, or your car got into trouble, or you hit awful bumper-to-bumper traffic. And, I will take a guess that you handled the situation similar to how I have in the past – you blamed someone else in the car with you for what went wrong. It's understandable. It is a natural human response to deflect the blame to others so we will not experience negative feelings of being wrong. However, you probably learned very quickly on your road trip the one major flaw with playing the blame game… it does nothing to solve the problem you're facing.

You see, we all have a tendency to cast blame for our problems. And this exposes a fatal flaw: *we view failure as an enemy.* However, if we shift our thinking to see failure not as an enemy, but as a friend, then suddenly we don't have to blame everyone anymore. Failure gives us a chance to grow. It exposes the places in our lives where we need to do some work and develop. Accepting responsibility for our actions, good or bad, empowers us and builds self-confidence.

Casting blame for our issues actually stops us from growing. It pushes us into the corners of fear and withdrawal. Just like on a road trip, casting blame doesn't solve the problem, it just annoys the other people in the car!

The best thing you can learn is that you are the common denominator of all your problems. Sure, it's not all your fault, but that doesn't really matter. What matters is that you take responsibility for the part that was your fault.

Growth happens when we are faced with challenge and adversity. No one grows while sipping drinks in the sun. As Thomas Edison famously put it regarding his string of failures in attempting to invent the light bulb: "I have not failed. I have just found 10,000 ways that won't work."

Failure is not your enemy; failure is your wise friend who comes alongside you in your journey and shows you how to become successful.

START BY ADDING VALUE FIRST, DON'T ASK WHAT THE MARKET CAN DO FOR YOU, ASK WHAT YOU CAN DO FOR THE MARKET

On January 20th, 1961, President John F. Kennedy gave his inaugural address. At the end of the speech, he famously uttered the phrase: "And so, my fellow Americans, ask not what your country can do for you, but what you can do for your country." It has gone down in history as one of the greatest political speeches in American history. Kennedy was calling on people to first ask how they can add value to the world, rather than sitting back and waiting on value to come to them.

This is also one of my favorite pieces of advice to give business owners and leaders who want to achieve success: stop asking what the market can do for you, look for what you can do for the market. Stop looking for the market to throw you a bone and help you out! Instead, focus your efforts on finding creative ways you can help the market.

For many of us, this means having a complete change of perspective about the marketplace. The marketplace is not simply where we go to make money and get rich. This view means that everyone else in the marketplace is just a stranger you hope to squeeze for a few dollars. I want you to view the marketplace and the world completely differently—everyone you meet is a friend who you can partner with!

At its core, the marketplace is a place where people come to exchange value. And many of us show up to the marketplace with our product, determined to sell it to as many people as we possibly can. This is the traditional model. But what if we changed that? What if instead of showing up with your product hoping people will fit your model, you showed up and tried to understand what challenges and issues people were having in the market? What if your main goal was to find ways to help people?

If you start by listening and understanding the pain and challenges that people face, you will start to figure out ways that you can help solve people's problems. And when you add that kind of value, value will return to you. Rather than chasing people around desperately asking them to buy your product, provide the products that will actually help people and they will start coming to you!

Stop asking the marketplace what it can do for you. Start finding out creative ways that you can add value and help the marketplace. In business, just as in life, karma rules. Whatever you put out into the world will come back to you. Add value and you will see value return to you.

CONCLUSION

In this chapter, I've given you a few strategies that can completely change your approach to your business, and even more importantly, your approach to your life. These are proven tactics that will get you to the places you want to be. There is nothing unique or special about simply wanting to be successful. In order to be successful, your desire has to be met with strategies and a plan on how to get there!

But, let's return one last time to our metaphor of a trip to the Grand Canyon. The truth is, you can put all the right strategies in place, you can be on the right road, with the right map, with a healthy car, etc. But, there will be plenty of times where you will look around and think, "I'm doing all the things I'm supposed to be doing but this doesn't look like the Grand Canyon!" There will be plenty of times where you will feel like you're headed the wrong direction, even though you're not.

The truth is, as important as desire and correct strategies are for finding the success you were meant to achieve are, there is one more thing that may actually be more important. Because without this the others will be meaningless, and that last thing is simply Perseverance.

On your journey towards success, there will be moments where you will feel like nothing is changing, like you're in the wrong place, or that you've made a huge mistake. You will question whether the Grand Canyon is actually worth it (it is!), or whether it's even possible to get to (it is!). And you can have all the right strategies in place, but if you don't have perseverance then they are useless.

So, I leave you with this thought: Don't give up! Don't give up on your dreams. Don't give up on your Grand Canyon. You can make it. With the desire in your heart, the right strategies for success, and the will to persevere and never give up, you can do anything!

About Fia

Fia Johannson is a producer, businesswoman, clinical hypnotherapist, author, visual artist, and even a psychic medium who works closely with police officers across the U.S. to help find missing people. Every aspect of her work is fueled by her belief that anyone can achieve anything they desire. Her life and rise to success is the greatest example of this notion. Throughout her career, she's literally helped thousands of people identify personal roadblocks in their lives and overcome them, paving their unique and fulfilling paths to success.

Some of Fia Johannson's accomplishments include speaking at the United Nations, as well as being featured in *Forbes*, *The Wall Street Journal*, CBS, NBC, ABC, and Fox News channels. Her greatest passion in life remains the ability to help others achieve their ultimate dreams and desires, teaching people to believe that truly, anything in this life is possible!

To connect with Fia:
- Instagram: @persianmedium
- Facebook: @persianmedium

Websites:
- www.persianmedium.com
- www.avidadvice.com

CHAPTER 11

THE EXTREME SPORT OF GRATITUDE

BY GRACE GREENLAND

When you think of an extreme sport, what is the first thing that comes to mind? Maybe it's someone surfing the biggest waves off the coast of Hawaii, or maybe it is a skier defying the laws of gravity as they glide and glisten through the air. What if I told you the most exciting and critical extreme sport in my life was gratitude? Yes, gratitude. When was the last time you were truly thankful for something? Thankful for anything? In my life, I have made it a personal mission to be thankful at all turns and crevices of my life, even if it's jotting down notes on a piece of paper lying around or a 'do not disturb' sign on the inside of my hotel room. Wherever there is a blank canvas and a willing and participating soul, a masterpiece can be created from the simplest of things.

I spent 14 years owning and operating a retail franchise in public works. It was hard, grueling work, but by practicing gratitude throughout my career, I am now able to travel the world and help others reach their full potential. I've found that there are four key strategies for actively achieving gratitude:

STRATEGY ONE: VISUALIZATION
BY PUTTING PEN TO PAPER

It is one thing to think you are going to do something, or think about the accomplishments and blessings in your life. It is a whole other entity entirely to sit down, put pen to paper and write down your thoughts, dreams, past accomplishments or future goals. How many times have you had such a deep and vivid dream that it almost seemed real and you didn't want it to end? ...only to wake up and remember maybe a quarter of what was happening, but you know there was so much more. When thoughts and ideas come to your mind about current or future success, why not remember them all? The one surefire way to make sure you never miss anything is simply to write them down. It's so simple but unbelievably effective. It forces the brain to work in more ways than one. It is one thing to think the thoughts in your mind and a whole other thing entirely to see those thoughts written down in front of you, your truths, your beliefs.

Seeing truly is believing. How will you know where to go, what to do, what to be thankful for if you have no plan? No baseline to grow from, no foundation to build upon through repetition and internal self-evaluation. A tactic that I embrace that has truly changed my life is writing and journaling as if the goal had already been achieved. Never would I have run a successful business for 14 years, or graduated as a mathematician or even traveled the world, had I not written my goals and aspirations down as if I had already achieved them. When you force yourself to visualize the end goal and make it become a part of your daily routine which you are seeing every day, you force yourself to have no choice but to reach your ultimate goals and dreams. It then becomes so much more attainable and a part of your normal.

STRATEGY TWO: TRUST THE PROCESS

Trust the process and trust that the achievement of the goal is coming. There is a process when getting from where you are to where you want to be. The easiest path and the path with less resistance may not always be the path for you; as much as we would love that to be true, life seems to always have its own plan for us. What you and I can do is prepare mentally and physically for our goals. How will we achieve our goals? Will you put in the necessary work and make the sacrifices needed to achieve those goals? I know it can be hard. I know sometimes after having a long, tough and strenuous day, the last thing that you want to talk, think, or write about is what you are grateful for and what work you will put in to achieve your goals.

Have you ever had one of those mornings where the last thing you wanted to do was go to the gym and exercise? 90% of the battle is just getting out the door. Once you've gotten out the door it seems so much less difficult and so much more achievable. I'm here to help you get up and get out that door. *This part is necessary. This part is critical.* Trust that your work will pay off. Trust that the masterpiece you are sculpting will turn out as beautiful and as amazing as you imagined.

The Name of The Game is Gratitude

The sport of gratefulness is just like any other sport, no one sees the countless hours you put in behind the scenes and how much work and dedication and sweat equity it took to get there. Elite athletes of the world spend more time training and preparing than they do playing the game. Why is this? They want to be as prepared mentally and physically as humanly possible. There are steps to everything, and without taking the appropriate steps how could you possibly expect there to be a payoff? Visualization leads to repetition and a structured process. Trust that process and push through even on the tough days. Your goals are attainable. Your dreams are reachable.

When the Going Gets Tough, The Tough Are Grateful

By now you have probably heard the same phrase over and over again, so much so that it begins to lose its true meaning. "If it was easy everyone would do it." The thing about gratitude is that it is easy and yes, in fact, everyone can do it. But how? How can I even begin to know what I'm grateful for? What does it even mean to be grateful for something? Isn't saying thank you enough? Gratefulness should be approached in a proactive sense and not a reactive sense. Be grateful for the journey. It is okay to try and fail at something, and when this happens it is essential to be persistent. Persistence truly is the key. Growth doesn't always occur in a straight and upward trending line, as much as we truly would love for that to happen. Sometimes a higher power has other plans for us, and we must be open, warm and receptive to the journey.

STRATEGY THREE: EMPOWERMENT

Sometimes our biggest obstacle is ourselves. You sometimes are the biggest roadblock in bringing more happiness, sanity, meaning, ease, and flow into your life. We have all been a victim of this at one point or another. We experience self-doubt and fear. Why do we let ourselves fall into the same routines over and over again and not allow ourselves to push forward and give full effort to achieving our goals? The answer is fear. Learn to overcome and overpower that fear through the use of visualization.

Act on it

Visualization? But haven't you said that already? Yes, I have, but there is another form of visualization. Instead of written visualization, there is the act of physical visualization. That is acting and living/pretending as if the dream life has already been achieved. When you write down what you're grateful for and visual it, every single day, after a while it becomes your reality. Start acting like it is your reality. Start acting like that new company you are opening is a massive success. Tell everyone about it, tell your neighbors, your peers and anyone that you know that it is a massive success. Once you firmly get behind your goals and believe in them why wouldn't everybody else? It is the human condition.

The applications for this train of thought are endless. If you believe it and give it 100%, what's stopping it from succeeding? You have to allow yourself to have success first and foremost before anyone else. Empower yourself and allow yourself the opportunity to succeed. Be your own biggest fan and open the door to yourself achieving all the things you've set out to achieve. If seeing is believing, then doing is achieving.

STRATEGY FOUR: TIE IT ALL TOGETHER

From step one to step two to step three, bringing everything together comes down to action. Taking action to practice gratitude is essential. One tool I've found to be extremely powerful in my own life is vision boarding. I organize international retreats to kickstart the power process of discovery through gratitude, and before I can organize an event at such a large scale, I must first organize my thoughts and goals.

Dream it, then do it

Vision Boarding is the perfect blend of reaching for the stars – and taking action. Vision boarding is a process where you go inside yourself, ask yourself what you want your life to look like, express it, then place your vision board in an area that you'll see every day, and draw inspiration from. Vision Boarding can be daunting at first, and I've found these steps to be a great guide when sitting down to Vision Board:

(i) – Dig Deep

First, find a quiet place where no one will disturb you. If you're a tactile learner, settle in with a notebook and pen. If you learn by processing out loud, find a place where you can talk to yourself and work through concepts by talking them over with yourself. Once you're ready to get started, ask yourself – what core values are important to you? Common core values include family comes first, believing in something bigger than yourself is important, and that happiness is a journey, not a destination. By identifying what you truly believe is important, then you can begin the work of vision boarding. Vision boarding will likely help you feel gratitude for your current life situation and where your life is going, because it helps unearth hidden desires and goals.

(ii) – Tap into Your Inner Child

The next step is to grab old magazines, newspapers and any other tactile elements that you think could inspire you. Be sure to keep yourself in check, don't select things just because they're visually appealing, it's okay to include things that you think fit your aesthetic, but it's necessary to keep an eye out for items that speak to you on a deeper level. Be on the lookout for items that align with your core values, and speak to the future life and success you're striving for.

It's also important to find a physical representation of your goals. If striving for a promotion at work, find elements that are tied to your job. If success for you is mending broken relationships, find words and pieces that speak love, forgiveness, and redemption. If you want to publish your own book, run a marathon or even change your diet – it can all start with visual representation through vision boarding. As you work through the process of discovering elements for your vision boarding, take time to jot down thoughts of gratitude as they come to you during the process.

(iii) – Bring Your Art to Life

After spending some time exploring your core values, interests and goals, bring the piece to life by either pasting magazine cutouts to a canvas, building something three-dimensional, or even painting or drawing your vision. Once your piece is finished, find a spot where you'll pass it every day and have a chance to reflect on it. Common places for vision boards include on the back of a bedroom door, in the bathroom or home office. You want this to be a place where you won't just walk by it, but take a moment to soak in the power of building your vision through art, and spend time being grateful for your goals and vision.

According to the Oxford dictionary, art is the expression or application of human creative skill and imagination, typically in a visual form such as painting or sculpture, producing works to be appreciated primarily for their beauty or emotional power. This means that your vision board will truly be art, and you must treat it as such.

Vision boarding is the final step because it brings vision and action together. Throughout the process of vision boarding, gratitude will likely come naturally. By spending time reflecting on who you are now, and who you want to be – you will have a chance to express gratitude for all events that led to your life as it is today, and you will have a chance to be grateful for the chance to build a successful future for yourself.

About Grace

Grace Greenland teaches motivation with Rhonda Byrne as one of her favorite authors, and follows the teachings of Michael Bernard Beckwith. She has attended Success Principles™ and Train The Trainer coaching events and luxury retreats with Jack Canfield. She has also worked with private coaching – with Janet Switzer, co-author of the book, *Success Principles*.

Grace's passion is to work with people, helping them discover the gift of their fullest potential, live their best life, for their highest good.

Grace has a business called TRANSFORMATIONAL WELLNESS & SUCCESS LUXURY MASTERMIND RETREATS. She run retreats all over the world for investors at exotic paradise locations, at top five-star luxury resorts, teaching people who are struggling how to get unstuck and how to get from where they are to where they want to be in life. She shows them how they can create the life they desire and deserve, in the supportive environment of her retreats, by 'start-designing' their best life and to start moving in the direction of their dream lifestyle – doing what they love – while earning fabulous income.

Grace Greenland graduated as a mathematician from university and traveled the world. She has owned and operated a retail franchise business in public service for 14 years. After selling her business, she completed graduate studies in Tibetan Buddhism for the Modern World in Sydney. Grace lived in Nepal extensively, traveling to Tibet, India and Bhutan as a spiritual practitioner, volunteer, sponsor and donor. She also teaches dharma in the Tibetan tradition.

Grace lives her life by the principles of Louise Hay and Doreen Virtue. Her interests in wellness are through meditation, mild yoga, chakras, nutrition, crystals and essential oils.

CHAPTER 12

BALANCED LIFE – SWEET SUCCESS

BY MICHELE HORNBY

I remember clearly the day the professionals at UCLA stated, "You will never be out of that wheelchair. Accept your life and move forward." That statement disturbed me. They didn't know me. They didn't know my life. And that statement did not resonate with my soul. I had been raised believing I was a daughter of God. I believed that, embraced that, and knew that God had instilled some of his divineness in me when I came to earth. Spending the rest of my life in bed or lying on a couch would not enable me to live the life God had intended for my life.

Two years previously, I had been diagnosed with multiple sclerosis at the age of 43. I was informed my case was very violent. I often lost the ability to walk within the first 12 hours of an exacerbation. The disease also affected my cognitive function, my vision, my speech, and control of basic bodily function. For the next eight years, I did everything the medical community recommended. I repeatedly lost the ability to walk, each time necessitating physical therapy to regain the ability to walk. During this time, I learned my body responded to natural treatments and therapies much better than prescribed, synthetic medicines. The side effects of the medicines were killing me. God continued guiding my path to increased knowledge on achieving wellness naturally. My amazing neurological team allowed my wishes to go natural in 2000 using natural plant-based medicines and, with a few stumbles, my health has improved dramatically.

Dis-Ease begins when an area of one's life is out of balance. Physical, mental, emotional, social, financial, and spiritual components contribute to our wholeness. If one is not mindful and in touch with their own physical body and any warning signals of pain or discomfort, an area can become so out of balance that chemical reactions change in the body, creating an environment of illness. Allostasis is the process of being mindfully aware of each area of your life and creating a homeostasis environment for your body. Stress and negativity not only affect your emotional and social condition, but dramatically affects your physical wellbeing. Lack of sleep or hydration not only affects the physical, but also the mental. Self-awareness and courage are needed to be fully in tune with your whole.

In the last 50 years, there has been a shift from 100% personal responsibility for one's health to putting the responsibility upon the doctor, the medical profession, the insurances, or even the government. A quick-fix mentality of "give-me-a-pill-to-fix-me" has led to powerful pharmaceutical companies and increased costs of medications. This has dramatically contributed to the decline of health. Added to this shift are the increased levels of chemicals in the environment and the food industry, and lifestyle changes such as more meals eaten outside of the home. Toxic insult to the human body has led to increased autoimmune diseases, stomach issues and synthetic medicine addictions.

Let's examine more closely what is needed to keep these six components of your whole being in balance:

1. **Physical** – Eat a diet composed mainly of organic healthy lean meats and fresh vegetables and fruit. Eating processed foods adds more toxins to the body in the form of

preservatives. Adequate hydration is essential to a healthy functioning body. Water, in the amount of half of your body weight in oz. (minimum of 64-80 oz.) is recommended to be consumed daily. This should include a full glass upon rising and a full glass of water before bed. Do not rely on caffeine or any other stimulus to motivate your brain. The inflammation resulting from artificial stimuli will result in increased mental fog and physical issues. Sleep is the time for your body to heal and reset. If you are not getting 7-8 hours of sleep each night, you are depriving your body of healing time and putting additional strain on your physical and mental function.

Natural vitamins and minerals supplements are strongly recommended now as our food and the American diet isn't meeting our nutritional requirements. The human body needs these elements to function optimally. Exercise or movement and being outside is recommended on a daily basis. Nature reminds us of the beauty of life. "Love and a sunset is all I need in life" is one of my favorite reminders of this.

Now let's examine our two minds: thinking and feeling:

2. **Mental** – Practice mindfulness and meditation daily. Take time for yourself every day. Engage in positive thoughts and be your own best coach, not critic. Remember the famous Dr. Wayne W. Dyer published Change Your Thoughts, Change your Life. Stay present in your daily relationships with non-judgmental observation. Stay away from toxic thoughts, toxic people and toxic conversations. Read something that lifts or inspires you daily. Manage your stress and your gut health. Remember the vagus nerve is the tenth cranial nerve which interacts with the parasympathetic control of the heart, lungs, and digestive tract. If your digestive and immune system is in flux, it will affect brain function which cascades into mental, emotional, and physical functions.

Practice gratitude. Attend yearly seminars or trainings that contribute to your mental wellness. Competence increases confidence. Commit to a lifetime of learning and improvement. Be clear on what you want out of life and always have a vision or dream to sustain you. Calendar this so that it doesn't get lost in worldly concerns.

3. **Emotional** – Mindfulness is the quest for all of us. Being loving and caring generates a higher level of energy. Compassion can change the world. *Be kind!* When you become aware of your current emotion, take a moment, feel it, identify it and be aware of what generated the emotion. Be in tune with your own emotional state. In business, remember not to take things personally. Everyone loves compliments; receiving criticism can be challenging. Look for the basis of truth in the critique and examine it for its merits. Jack Canfield says, "Use feedback to your advantage." Have a support team of trusted and respected friends or professionals who can be there to support and guide you in rough times. Remember those rough patches lead to learned lessons and increased resilience. Do not use food or drink as crutches for emotional stress. That habit will only throw the physical aspect of your life also out of balance.

4. **Spiritual** – Spiritual balance is essential, no matter your personal beliefs. Acquiring a spiritual practice is associated with better health and well-being. Discernment of truths and decisions based on a moral code of beliefs will guide you to be the best person you can be. Gratitude for the blessings of your life will bring greater joy and happiness to each day. Generosity with your time and means allow you to give back to others. Service allows greater joy in allowing one to get out of their own life and help others. Meditating calms your mind, quiets the ego and opens awareness to personal revelation. Affirmations claim unlimited power from the universe and assist in removing subconscious blocks that hinder our personal growth and movement. Let go and let

God is a popular idiom used for drawing on higher powers to guide our lives.

5. **Social** – Know thyself. Be nonjudgmental, friendly, don't try to fix others. Remember to associate with people who lift you up. Don't be a "flake." Honor commitments and respect others. Have fun, laugh, be with people you can relax with and be stimulated and encouraged by. Avoid screen time and engage in more people time. Appreciate yourself and all others. Being kind generates joy. Nurture relationships and rekindle old friendships with people who are respectful, positive and supportive.

6. **Financial** – Stress caused from financial concerns harms relationships, causes emotional anxiety, often leading to depression and increased inflammation in the physical body. If one lives within their means, remembering to always pay yourself or save money every check, this stress can be eliminated. Study how to be financially savvy. Avoid paying interest. Be aware of money habits and attitudes learned from parents and grandparents. Are these habits and attitudes serving you?

When life is balanced, all your energy and creativity can be directed towards your success. Always be open to learning and improvement. A simple exercise done quarterly will assist your recognition of balance in your life. Ask yourself, "If I were to take 10% more responsibility for my health, what are three things I am willing to commit to do?" List those three items and then ask the same question on each of the following areas: mental, emotional, spiritual, social and financial health. Then calendar those goals into your weekly schedule. They are as important as any business call or update. When balanced, one is more focused, clear, and happy. This contributes greatly to business success.

LIFE IN BALANCE
Avoid Dis-Ease - Address Any Stress

If I were to take 10% more responsibility for my mental health, I would:

1._____
2._____
3._____

If I were to take 10% more responsibility for my physical health, I would:

1._____
2._____
3._____

If I were to take 10% more responsibility for my financial health, I would:

1._____
2._____
3._____

If I were to take 10% more responsibility for my spiritual health, I would:

1._____
2._____
3._____

If I were to take 10% more responsibility for my social health, I would:

1._____
2._____
3._____

If I were to take 10% more responsibility for my emotional health, I would:

1._____
2._____
3._____

Concept taught by Tiffanyspeaks.com and Jack Canfield

Life is beautiful! I have a great life. Others might look at my life and regret such a hard life. Chronic illness and widowed so young, but in finding my truth, I have found my life is an opportunity for growth, learning and development. Multiple sclerosis made me a better person, being widowed made me a stronger person, running businesses made me a more intelligent and compassionate being.

When I am balanced, I am happy and well, and continue to expand upon this lovely life. May we all work daily towards 100% personal responsibility and being balanced, so we may be healthy and enjoy living this beautiful life.

A life well-lived is true success.

About Michele

Raised in Swan Valley, Idaho, Michele Hornby is a graduate of the University of Utah where she received her Master's in Gerontology, a BA in Psychology from Brigham Young University along with an AA degree in Accounting. She has worked in Washington, D.C., Sydney, Australia, and Los Angeles, CA.

Her last two degrees were obtained after the diagnosis of multiple sclerosis. The return to school was in an effort to regain cognitive functioning due to losses caused by her first MS exasperation. Michele was the Utah Valley Volunteer of the year in 1997 and the Utah State MS Champion of the Year in 1998. This honor included being present at signing the MS official day declaration with Governor Mike Levitt. The National Multiple Sclerosis Society awarded her a Lifetime Achievement Award in 1999.

Michele is a passive partner in Sleepy J Cabins, LLC and owner of Authentic Health, LLC. Besides being a natural Health Educator, she is an international speaker and author. She was just featured on "Hollywood Live" with Jack Canfield which will hit airwaves this fall.

Mother of three and a grandmother of five, Michele currently resides in Queen Creek, Az. She is widowed. Her husband, Glen Hornby, was a police officer and detective for the Los Angeles Police Dept.

Michele's personal experience with the medical community led to her passion for wellness and the use of natural plants, diet and exercise to achieve and maintain a homogeneous environment for life.

As an engaging international speaker, Michele loves helping others recognize the power of positive, mindful living.

Check out Michele's website at: AuthenticHealthUSA.com
   or
Contact Michele at: AuthenticHealthUSA@aol.com

CHAPTER 13

THE SCIENCE OF SUCCESS

BY STACEY O'BYRNE

I have been working with entrepreneurs, business owners and sales people for over twenty years and the one common factor they all share is the pursuit of success. Some find it easy to achieve, while others encounter roadblocks through their journey towards success, and then there are others that never hit their desired goals and they get frustrated and give up. I have always been a personal and professional development junkie, and seminar-after-seminar and workshop-after-workshop, I have always heard the same philosophy, that success is easy. Although I agree with that philosophy, I do believe that there is a little bit more to it; success is achievable by all as long as they embrace the fact that success is a science. As with any science there are steps to achieving a desired outcome.

All my life, success has been relatively easy. At times it has come with its challenges, and there have definitely been times when I have fallen hard and desperately wanted to give up, but chose to keep plugging forward. I have invested the past 20 years mastering the science of success both for myself and to help others.

Looking back on my own life, I've realized that I always did well in school. I always made the all-star team for softball and basketball. When I was in the Army, I was awarded Soldier of the Quarter and Soldier of the Year. When I worked in Corporate America, I excelled in every job I had, and climbed the ranks of success quickly and easily in every job I ever had. Since I have ventured off on my own journey as an entrepreneur 20 years ago, I have built successful businesses, and today I own eight (8) thriving, successful businesses, one of which is a seven-figure business, several others are six-figure businesses, and one other one is a new venture we just recently started with a very exciting potential upside.

All of these experiences of success have helped me realize that the common denominator in my successes and my unsuccessful endeavors is always me, and the reality is that it is so much deeper. There really were, and still are, key factors involved in achieving success. I've come to understand that where I go, I follow, and through that understanding how I choose to show up directly impacts the results I achieve, good or bad. I've come to understand that there are five (5) major key factors, and that as long as I stay true to them, I can achieve whatever I want very easily and effortlessly.

1. The first Key Factor is clarity.

Have you ever noticed that when you ask someone what they want, one of two things happens? They will either tell you what they don't want, or they answer the question very ambiguously. There are a few obvious problems with this. The first problem is the most obvious. When we focus on what we don't want, that is exactly what we create, and our energy goes where our focus flows. So, when someone can immediately tell you what they don't want to happen, it's pretty clear that is where their focus and energy are directed. The next is the not-so-obvious problem, ambiguity. We need very clear, specific direction. Think about it, if you wanted to go on vacation but didn't know where you wanted to go, how successful would you be at planning a vacation?

As a matter of fact, the average person spends more time planning their vacations than they do their success. It is very important for you to have specific clarity on what it is you want. Instead of saying you want more money, clarify with how much specifically, and by when specifically. I jokingly tell people if you focus on more money and you find a penny, as far as your brain is concerned, you have achieved your objective. The word more is a comparative, and the first thing our mind does is ask compared to what? ...compared to what you have now? Have complete specific clarity on what it is you want, and that is the first key factor to achieving your desired success.

2. The second Key Factor to achieving success is being at cause.

We have multiple choice points in our pursuit of success and there is one that is a very clear, debilitating sabotage that very few rarely see without a struggle, and that is, we are either the cause of our situations or the effect. This is a very sour pill to swallow, and I invite you to be open through this. I have a belief that we can either have reasons/excuses, or we can have results, but it is impossible to have both. This belief has served me well through my whole life. Whenever I have had excuses, I quickly noticed I never achieved what I set out to accomplish, and whenever I stayed focused on my outcome and adjusted how I "showed up" and participated in the results, I always achieved what I set out to accomplish.

Instead of looking to blame, look to adjust what isn't working and make adjustments accordingly. Remember you are the common denominator in your life, so if you aren't getting the results you wanted, adjust how you are participating. I get a lot of pushback with this philosophy and I promise you, if you allow yourself to embrace this key factor and look inwards at yourself and never externally, your pursuit of success will be so much easier. Look! That doesn't mean that life isn't going to happen, and that there will never be external circumstances that create obstacles, it just means when you stay results-focused and adapt and adjust accordingly, removing any and all excuses, then results become inevitable.

3. The third Key Factor to achieving success is our imagination.

The biggest mistake we ever made was we grew up. We stopped allowing ourselves to daydream. Remember the first key factor was clarity, understanding specifically what we want. It is important to be able to use our imagination to create a sensory-based visual representation of what we want once we have our clarity. Remember, our energy goes where our focus flows.

Allow yourself to imagine what it will look like while you are achieving your success. What sounds are associated with it? Imagine what you would say to yourself and what you would think while you are achieving your desired success. Close your eyes for a moment and allow yourself to be in that moment, as if you are living in that moment, feeling it with every ounce of yourself, seeing it with your own eyes, thinking to yourself what you would be thinking. What are you hearing at that very moment when you have accomplished what you set out to accomplish? If you can attach all your senses to the pursuit of your success and achieving it, then you can go after it with all you have.

4. The fourth Key Factor to achieving success is a plan.

You've heard the old adage, if you fail to plan then you plan to fail. Allow yourself to invest time to plan your success. It's important to understand your starting point as well as the specifics of what it is you want to accomplish, your success. Next, you want to share your desired outcome with a support team: coaches, masterminds, referral partners and anyone else that is like-minded and shares similar success dreams with you.

Now block out some time to develop a roadmap, those actions need to be taken to achieve your desired success. After you have all of that figured out, schedule out everything you just mapped out, and then put your plan and schedule into action.

A few things to keep in mind with planning for success. You *must*, must take action on your plan, and while you are taking action on your plan, always reflect on where you are and what you've accomplished, continually educate yourself to ensure you have all the resources necessary to achieve your desired success and continually utilize laser-focused sensory acuity to ensure that you stay on course, and if necessary, allow yourself the behavioral flexibility to course correct. The Titanic was 1° (one degree) off course and the outcome was tragic; continually utilizing sensory acuity and flexibility will allow you to easily course correct when necessary. While you are working your plan, remember success is a journey, it is not a destination.

5. <u>The fifth Key Factor to achieving success is mindset.</u>

Mindset in itself is a huge concept and when combined with the other key factors, is completely life changing. In order to master mindset, we must first understand what it is and where it comes from. Science has proven that we have been imprinted between birth and the age of seven (7) by significant adult figures in our lives. We are imprinted with everything we need to know in every area of life, relationships, money, communication, health, work ethic, spirituality, our environment, and much, much more. Looking at your currently reality and your successes, or maybe your lack thereof in these areas, by our parents, aunt and uncles, grandparents, siblings and in some cases, friends, parents of friends, teachers and neighbors.

Think about the areas of your life that are thriving, how were those same areas for you in your life growing up and with the significant adults in your life? Typically, people thrive where the adults in their life thrived, and struggle in the same areas of their life where the significant adults struggled. It is because that is how we were imprinted, programmed to respond in specific areas and to have specific relationships with specific behaviors. Our brain is the operating system for our life, it was programmed early on how to live and how to do "things." Like any programming, it serves a specific purpose. However, over time, the program becomes outdated and no longer serves the purpose of its environment.

The good news is that, just like with computers and software, all programs can be reprogrammed – updated, so to speak – to serve its newer environment. Those old adages that say, "If you think you can, you can, and if you think you can't, you can't – either way you're right," and, "If you change the way you look at the world, then the world around you changes" are absolutely right, they are simplified explanations of how important our mindset is, and how our mindset impacts our life.

Our mindset doesn't define our life, our mindset determines our life. The majority of entrepreneurs I have met when I speak at events struggle financially and they just get by. Most of us today have either been raised by people who lived through the Great Depression, or were raised by people who were raised by people who lived through that era. Money was very scarce during that time period, and a scarcity mindset and fear around money developed. Then those same people unknowingly passed that mindset on to their loved ones throughout generations that followed, through very innocent comments like, "Honey, we can't afford that." or, "You have to save for a rainy day." or, "Money is the root of all evil." or some other innocent statement that alluded to money not being abundant. So, many innocent comments rapidly grow in our minds to mean different things as we get older, and the major underlying result is a scarcity mindset, or the inability to prosper easily or even acceptance that we are unable to afford what we want.

So, allow yourself to have a mindset of success and abundance. Allow yourself to embrace the reality that if you believe that we live in a world where anything is possible, then that means we live in a world where everything is possible. Remember the brain that created your 'today' is incapable of creating a different 'tomorrow.' Allow yourself to reprogram the mindset that has created the today that excludes the success you want, to the mindset of creating the tomorrow that you have always desired and deserved.

When you realize that success is truly a science, allow yourself to learn and embrace the science of success. Success is easy, you just have to get out of your own way to allow success to happen. Always remember, choice is a powerful thing and suffering is optional.

Allow yourself to dream, plan to take action, believe you can, and keep a mindset that supports your successful desires and always goes for it and gives it everything you have. Shoot for excellence and avoid mediocrity. I look forward to hearing about all your successes that you allow yourself to create.

NOW GO MAKE THIS SHIFT HAPPEN!

About Stacey

Stacey O'Byrne is an international speaker, trainer, author and co-author of several books, a certified NLP Master Trainer, owns multiple franchises, is a dedicated serial entrepreneur and a U.S. Army Veteran.

Stacey has built two seven-figure businesses and two six-figure businesses 100% from word-of-mouth marketing. Stacey has worked with thousands of entrepreneurs, helping them create the success they desire and deserve.

Stacey O'Byrne has over 20 years' experience as a successful sales professional, manager, leader, business owner and entrepreneur. She has a diversified professional background, which has enhanced her trainings and allows her to offer a broad range of expertise to her clients.

Stacey is a graduate of San Diego State University. She is the President and CEO of Pivot Point Advantage, a training company specializing in NLP (Neuro-Linguistic Programming), Sales, Leadership, Advanced Communications and Success Strategies.

Her training in the military, a strong background in sales and management in the Corporate world, and her successful journey as a business owner and entrepreneur, have helped her develop a strong understanding of the challenges that today's professionals experience. She understands the value in personal and professional development, and how it directly influences one's performance as a salesperson, client advocate, business owner or professional.

Stacey is passionate about helping sales professionals, business owners and entrepreneurs learn that through the right mindset, effective goal-setting, strategizing, planning, accountability, and effective coaching, they can increase productivity and accomplish tasks and goals that previously seemed out of reach. It is her intention to help them learn how to design their destiny and live the life they've always dreamed of, desired and deserve.

Stacey's passion in life is seeing others live their dreams. If you would like to connect with Stacey or share your accomplishments, please do so.

You can connect with Stacey at:
- www.pivotpointadvantage.com
- stacey@pivotpointadvantage.com
- www.facebook.com/staceyobyrne
- www.linkedin.com/staceyobyrne

CHAPTER 14

DIVORCE WITH DIGNITY

BY LISA ZARKIN MCHUGH

I'm not going to pretend to be an expert in the field of divorce. However, I have done it twice and it is not my intention to do it again. The first time was what I like to call a mulligan, and something I don't talk about much. I'm not sure that using this common golf term is a proper word for the divorce world, but I was young and like to think of it as the universe giving me another chance. Some people might look at it as a failure, but I look at it as a life lesson and a way to help other people. Plus, I believe I have learned more from my failures than I have from my successes. As a CERTIFIED FINANCIAL PLANNER™ and life coach, I have worked with many people before, during and after their divorces. I have helped them by actively listening to their thoughts, fears and needs while offering creative advice which allows them to realize their dreams. Going through a divorce can give you a new perspective and sometimes that is just what people need to get them on the right track.

One thing to remember when you are going through a divorce is that it doesn't have to be hard and it should always be done with dignity. What I mean by that is you can go through a divorce while remaining respectful to your spouse, children, and most importantly, to yourself. I grew up with loving parents who were married for almost 61 years until my father passed away. He was a high school English and History teacher and my mother was a stay at home mom. They managed to survive having eight children, with me being the last. When I was three years old, my mother started working in the financial industry. She was a brilliant woman who could do anything she set her mind to. She was very intuitive and artistic, and she had a knack for helping people. As a CERTIFIED FINANCIAL PLANNER™ she quickly rose to the top of a mostly male-oriented industry with her unique and creative advice. Do you think my mother had an easy time staying balanced through all of this? The answer is of course, no. So how was my mother able to raise eight children, remain mostly happy, married and have a successful career? The answer is she always had a positive attitude and she never spoke badly about anyone.

My mother used to always tell me about positive thinking, and she would say, "There is no need to worry because the universe will bring you money." As a kid, I thought she was crazy, but as the years went on, I started to understand what she meant. Our thoughts are extremely powerful, and we create what we think. We must be intentional about what we want and what we think about. Although I don't usually tell clients that the universe will bring them money, I do incorporate the law of attraction and positive thinking into my meetings. What does any of this have to do with divorcing with dignity? It has everything to do with it!

My childhood was happy. I had a great relationship with my parents who were both loving and supportive. Despite all of that, I still ended up divorced. My parents were two completely different individuals. My mother was the caring, gentle and positive type who worked hard, but also had a very independent side. My father was also loving and caring, but he didn't express it in the same ways my mother did. He didn't talk about feelings or say "I love you" like my mother did, but he showed it in other ways. For example, he would read to me every morning and he would sit with me in his chair and play me his music. I remember those giant headphones he would place over my head while blasting the Eagles, Bob Segar, Queen and so much more. My point is that most women and men express their love in many different ways to each other and their children, and sometimes I wondered why my parents were together at all. There are many reasons why people choose to get divorced, and too many times it ends in an expensive battle that can leave all those involved bitter and resentful.

Life brings many lessons and we choose how we react to these lessons. We can't control anyone or anything; we can only control how we react to the situation. If you choose divorce, here are some steps and examples of how to do it with dignity before, during, and after.

1. Speak kindly about your spouse or don't say anything at all

We have all heard the quote, "If you don't have anything nice to say, don't say anything at all." This is true for divorce! It's not anyone else's business why you are getting divorced and you don't need to come up with an excuse. This is between you and your spouse. If you have children, sure, you may need to give them a reason, but it isn't anyone else's business.

I know a lot of people going through a divorce don't want to feel like they have failed, so they like to put the blame on the other person. Be the bigger person and take responsibility. After all it takes two people to get married and it takes two people to get divorced. You are each 100% responsible for the choices you make. Even if you think you have always been the perfect example of a spouse, it doesn't make you look better when you speak badly about anyone else. Especially when it's someone you've been living with for 10, 15, 20 or more years. Not only that, but if you chose to have children with this person, they don't want to hear bad things about their parent and believe me; it will get back to them. Plus, it's just bad energy and you don't want to bring that energy to yourself.

2. Avoid hypocrisy

I can't tell you how many times I have heard people complain about their spouse and how they did this and they did that and how terrible they are, etc., etc., yet at the same time, these people have been having affairs for years. These feelings and things about your spouse may be true. Hell, he or she might be the worst, most evil person in the world, but people don't believe you when you have been dishonest yourself. Can you say HYPOCRITE? Also, if you are thinking about having an affair because you aren't happy, communicate with your spouse or a professional, talk it out, or get divorced, but don't have an affair. It will only cause resentment and it will make it nearly impossible to have an amicable or inexpensive divorce.

3. Take stock of the people in your life

Take some time to think about the people in your life and how you feel around them. You are going through a big change and sometimes people can't handle change. This usually stems from their own fears and really has nothing to do with you. If someone you thought was a friend isn't there for you anymore because you are going through a divorce, ask yourself if they ever really were a friend. If the answer is no, then these are the people you can weed out of your life. Remember that emotions run high for everyone involved and sometimes people need time to adjust. Talk to a professional about your emotions and don't expect your friends to take on that role.

4. Take time for yourself

This is an emotional time and a huge amount of change. You will be sad even if it's something you've been thinking about for years. Feel your feelings and talk to a professional or join a support group. Learn how to meditate, do some self-help courses and read self-help books. Don't keep everything bottled inside. If you don't work on your feelings, you will continue to make the same mistakes in future relationships. Most importantly, it's okay to have fun and not feel guilty.

5. Take time to be with your children

It is important to communicate with your children. Let them know you love them and that your divorce has nothing to do with them. Take time to be with them all together as well as individually. No matter what their age, this is a loss for them. It is a major change and it is scary. They will need to know that you will always love them and will always be there for them no matter what. Change is inevitable and they will be stronger for it as long as you show them love and respect.

6. Communicate respectfully and work out as much as you can together before meeting with an attorney

If your spouse is willing, set a time to go through your finances and decide a co-parenting arrangement before you meet with an attorney. If your spouse isn't willing to work out the details, then do it alone or with the help of a CERTIFIED FINANCIAL PLANNER™. Then you can present your spouse with a respectful and fair proposal. As hard as it might be, try not to act out of emotion. You may be feeling like you want to take everything they own, but this is acting out of what we call the three R's. They are resentment, resistance and revenge. Is it really the fair thing to do and will you feel good about your actions in the next month, year or years? Plus, it might be impossible to come to an agreement if you aren't reasonable. The more you can agree upon before meeting with an attorney, the more you will save in time and fees.

7. Be respectful to each other in front of the children

Please do not fight in front of the children! Your children love both of you and they do not want to see you fight. They may take it personally and harbor resentment. If you can't get along then stay away from each other when the children are around, or until you cool down.

8. Realize what is important to you and be happy

Don't give up your home if you absolutely love it, but if it's going to strap you down and make you miserable, keeping you up at night wondering how you are going to make the next payment, sell it or let your spouse keep it. Nothing is worth all that stress. I gave up my home to create a calmer environment for me and my children. No monetary stuff is worth more than you or your children's wellbeing. Being happy means being balanced and to me that means no stress, seeing my children happy and having time with them and myself.

9. Hire an attorney that you feel comfortable with

The attorney you hire needs to be someone you feel comfortable with since you may be spending a lot of time and money with them. You may also be discussing some of the most intimate parts of your life, so make sure you like him or her. Make sure they take the time to explain things and that you understand how they invoice for email, phone, court, documents, etc.

If you need additional documents drafted such as a Qualified Domestic Relations Order (QDRO), will that be included in their services, or will you need to hire another attorney to draft it? I've had clients whose ex-spouses were so bitter from the divorce that they didn't want to retire because they didn't want their spouses to get a dime of their pensions. They literally said, "I would rather die than see them get a penny of my retirement." So, rather than retiring and collecting their pensions, they ended up miserable and working until they died. This can happen, so make sure you work with someone who understands QDRO's. If you don't ask the questions now, you might pay for it later!

10. Meet with a CERTIFIED FINANCIAL PLANNER™ (CFP®) if you haven't yet

The end of a marriage is also the beginning of a new financial life. Reconsidering your financial arrangements should be a priority as you adjust to your new circumstances. Find a CERTIFIED FINANCIAL PLANNER™ who you connect with. They can help you plan for your future and offer advice on your new financial situation. Ask them how they get paid—fee, commission, hourly, etc. Do not be afraid to ask questions!

The decision to divorce is not an easy one, but if you choose it, remember that you are strong, and you are worthy of happiness. It's important to look forward and let go of the past. Keep a positive attitude and love yourself. Give yourself grace and don't try to do everything alone. You are a huge influence and a hero in many people's lives. Inspire others to be brave, even in the most challenging situations. When you do this, you will have more abundance, love and success in all aspects of your life!

DISCLOSURES

About Lisa

For over 20 years, Lisa Zarkin McHugh has been dedicated to her career in the financial industry. After obtaining her Securities and Insurance licenses, Lisa and her mother, Diane, formed PlanSmart Financial Services, Inc.

In order to further her financial education, Lisa obtained a BA in Business from DePaul University and her CFP® certification in 1998. Lisa's top priority is helping clients set and work towards their goals while providing trustworthy, experienced advice with integrity and personal service. Lisa offers top-tier guidance to clients of high-net-worth, successful professionals, business owners, retirees and more. In addition to financial planning, Lisa runs a full-service tax planning and preparation firm through PlanSmart Financial Services, Inc. She specializes in financial planning before, during and after divorce. Lisa was listed in *Chicago Magazine* in 2018 and 2019 as a winner of the Five Star Professional Award as a financial advisor. For more information, please visit: www.plansmartfinancial.com.

Lisa is the author of the young adult book series, *Layla Bali*. The first book under the series is titled, *Layla Bali, A Rainbow in the Dark*, and the second novel coming soon titled, *Layla Bali and the Dream Catcher*. She and her books were featured on the Kate Delaney Radio Program in the summer of 2019. More information about the book series can be found at: www.LaylaBaliBook.com.

As an entrepreneur, Lisa has owned and operated the children's haircare line called Zoo On Yoo. Zoo On Yoo has been creating and manufacturing haircare products since 2007, and currently wholesale's their products around the country.

Lisa is an avid contributor to many charitable organizations including the 501(c)(3) non-profit charity she formed in 2014 called All Life Animal Rescue. Lisa's goal is to form a foundation which gives grants and donations to many charities with a focus on animals, children (especially special needs and childhood cancer), and veterans.

Lisa has served on the Board of Giving DuPage since 2016. Giving DuPage is a charitable organization that connects volunteers with charitable organizations in the DuPage County area. Lisa has also served as the Chair of the Giving DuPage's Volapalooza event since 2016. Volapalooza is an annual event which honors volunteers and volunteerism in the community.

Lisa resides in Naperville, IL with her husband and three children. In her spare time, she plays tennis with the Northern Illinois Traveling Tennis League as well as the United States Tennis Association.

Disclosures: